YOUNG OFFENDER

Michael Maisey

PAN BOOKS

First published 2019 by Pan Books
an imprint of Pan Macmillan
20 New Wharf Road, London N1 9RR
Associated companies throughout the world
www.panmacmillan.com

ISBN 978-1-5290-0547-9

Copyright © Michael Maisey 2019

The right of Michael Maisey to be identified as the
author of this work has been asserted by him in accordance
with the Copyright, Designs and Patents Act 1988.

All rights reserved. No part of this publication may be reproduced,
stored in a retrieval system, or transmitted, in any form, or by any means
(electronic, mechanical, photocopying, recording or otherwise)
without the prior written permission of the publisher.

Pan Macmillan does not have any control over, or any responsibility for,
any author or third-party websites referred to in or on this book.

1 3 5 7 9 8 6 4 2

A CIP catalogue record for this book is available from the British Library.

Typeset by Palimpsest Book Production Limited, Falkirk, Stirlingshire
Printed and bound by CPI Group (UK) Ltd, Croydon, CR0 4YY

This book is sold subject to the condition that it shall not, by way of
trade or otherwise, be lent, hired out, or otherwise circulated without
the publisher's prior consent in any form of binding or cover other than
that in which it is published and without a similar condition including
this condition being imposed on the subsequent purchaser.

Visit **www.panmacmillan.com** to read more about all our books
and to buy them. You will also find features, author interviews and
news of any author events, and you can sign up for e-newsletters
so that you're always first to hear about our new releases.

YOUNG OFFENDER

Michael Maisey was born and raised in Isleworth and became one of London's most prolific young lawbreakers. Twenty years after the armed robbery that changed his life, he is now sober, the proud father of two daughters and the owner of an estate-agency business. As well as being an aspiring actor, he dedicates his spare time to mentoring young offenders and addicts and was recently honoured by the London Borough of Hounslow for his services to the community. You can follow Michael on Instagram, Facebook and Twitter @MichaelMaisey.

EAST SUSSEX COUNTY COUNCIL
WITHDRAWN
2 1 MAY 2024
27

04604016

I dedicate this book to anyone who has been affected by, or lost their life to, addiction or alcoholism, or is battling with their mental health, has been bullied, is sitting in a prison cell without hope, has experienced any form of abuse, is growing up in a broken home or has a parent suffering from addiction or alcoholism, and to all those in recovery and fighting the good fight to become a better version of themselves every day.

Prologue

Looking up at the red-brick walls I once knew so well, I feel a familiar quickening of my heartbeat. The last time I left this place, I swore I would never come back. But here I am again, though every cell in my body is telling me to turn around and run while I still can. What am I doing here? Why would I put myself through this? They're going to tear me apart.

My friend Luke puts his hand on my shoulder and squeezes.

'You all right, mate?' he asks.

I nod but I can't find the words.

'We need to get inside,' he says.

Inside. Again. But this time I'm walking through a different entrance. It's been nine years since I was last here. I was still a teenager then. Now I'm twenty-seven and it's sixteen months since I last had a drink or drugs. My life is better than I ever dreamed it could be. Everything is different now. I've got my own home, a good job, a great supportive girlfriend in Hayley. My future is secure. Yet the thought of going back into this building scares me in a way I never expected.

The guards barely look at me when they take my ID at the

1

security check. If they recognize my face or my name, they don't show it.

'You know where you're going?' one of them asks Luke.

'Wren,' he says.

A pretty name for an ugly place.

All the wings at Feltham are named after birds. Birds that don't normally end up in cages. There's Lapwing, the induction unit, where new inmates spend their first night inside getting used to how the institution works. Then there's Quail, for those convicted of the most violent crimes. Wren, where we're going today, is the healthcare wing where inmates with substance abuse problems and addictions are taken care of. Wren. A tiny bird with a hopeful little tail. Setting for the worst days of my life.

And I'm going back in there.

I follow Luke down the corridor. I lag behind a little. It's like my body is still resisting this return to the scene of the crime. I remember this corridor only too well. The alternating panels of bars and blank brick walls. The blast of cold air as we walk through the barred parts, which are open to the outside. I breathe it in. It's better than the smell inside. Old dinners, body odour, desperation. It takes me right back and not in a good way.

Luke is walking fast now. We're running late and nothing runs late in a place like this without consequences. But I want this moment in the corridor to last a little longer. I need more time to get myself together. Get ready to make my entrance. I don't think Luke understands how important that will be. In those first few seconds everything will be decided.

'This is going to be good,' Luke assures me. 'I can't think of anyone better suited to talking to this lot than you are.'

I want to believe him but then I catch a glimpse of myself in a toughened glass panel and I know exactly how they're going to see me. Who's that idiot in the designer jeans? What's his hair *like*? Who does he think he is?

Pretty little white boy.

I hear the hiss of angry voices I thought I'd long forgotten.

You gonna die, pretty boy. You gonna die.

The guard who lets us onto Wren raises his eyebrows when he sees me. He remembers me and he nods his approval, though he stops short of shaking my hand. I don't have time to remind myself if he was one of the good ones. There were some good ones. A couple who actually seemed to care. Luke is rushing me on.

Then it happens. As we walk onto the wing, I glance right. I can't help it. It's automatic. And the cell I see there makes me catch my breath. The door is open like a hungry mouth and suddenly I'm falling back through time. I can hear the alarm and the shouting and feel the panic as clearly as if the past nine years haven't happened. I can feel the shaking and the shivering. My skin is crawling again. The voices won't stop talking. They're talking to me now.

You're a piece of shit. Nobody here cares what happens to you. Why are you even alive?

Luke notices I'm distracted and yanks me back into the present.

'Michael. They're waiting for us. Come on.'

He pulls me along with him.

Sixteen inmates are already sitting in the middle of the wing on a circle of grey plastic chairs. There are two empty seats. One for Luke. One for me. As we approach, the inmates start heckling. Clicking their tongues. Cussing under their breath. *Pretty little white boy.* Who am I? What have I got to say to them? As Luke introduces me I start to size them up, reverting to my old survival techniques. I should know how to handle this. I've been here. My old defence mechanisms kick into action and I give myself the talk. I go through my audience one by one, rating my chances.

You could have him. You could have him too. He's full of shit. He'd never fight . . .

The inmates stare at me and I stare right back. We're like dogs now. Guessing at each other's strength. Bluffing. Hackles up. Who's going to slink away first? They slouch in their chairs. They talk among themselves. They want me to understand that they don't care why I'm here. They don't care who I am. Nothing I have to say is going to be relevant to them. Nothing I say is going to make a difference. I'm just like all the others. Coming in here to make *myself* feel better. Don't mean shit to them what some white boy in designer jeans with his hair all nice and styled has to say about what they're going through.

But I know you, I silently tell them. *I know you all.*

Luke asks them to welcome me. I think he's about to go for a round of applause. He thinks better of it, thank God. The hissing and the clicking get louder.

Fucking stupid white boy . . .

They know they can say what they want in here. There are no guards at this meeting. It's like any other twelve-step gathering. It's anonymous. What they say now, they say in confidence.

4

It stops here. Those are the rules. For half of them, that's the only attraction.

Pretty little white boy . . . don't know fuck . . .

The open cell door is still nearby. I could turn and walk through it. Close it. Sink down onto the floor with a blanket tight around my neck and this time see it through. I can feel it. My body remembers. The rising blackness. The pain. The fear. The faces of my loved ones flashing through my brain as I struggled for a last breath. My conscious mind fights to take back control.

You are different now, it reminds me. *You're not that boy. You can do this.*

I straighten up. The people in front of me are just kids. They're in the high-dependency unit of a young offenders institution. They're not here because they know what they're doing with their lives. They're all here because they fucked up. Some of them are barely conscious. They can't focus on what's in front of them. They're here because they need help. I can give them that. I can tell them what recovery really means.

I look straight at the kid who's been giving the most lip, then I turn to point at the open door.

'You see that cell?' I ask. 'Nine years ago, that's where I almost succeeded in taking my own life.'

The mouthy kid looks confused. Someone else laughs. I nod at them.

'Yep. That's right. I was in here three times. Robbery, assault, attempted murder . . .'

The circle is silent. I've got their attention now.

'I was here,' I say, 'and it nearly fucking killed me. So don't tell me I don't know what it's like.'

Now they're listening. The kid who looked like he'd be the most trouble leans forward in his chair.

As he does so, I can feel the rope of memory unwinding itself from around my neck. I take another breath and this time it properly fills my lungs. I'm still here. I'm still alive. The door of the empty cell closes softly and this time I'm on the outside.

'It doesn't have to be like this,' I begin.

I

I was born in Ashford, Middlesex, in the summer of 1982. It should have been a fairy-tale beginning. My parents, Teresa and Kevin Wright, were hopelessly in love. Almost forty years on from when she first met him, Mum still claims to love my dad, though these days he's far from the long-haired Prince Charming she met in 1979. He was her first proper sweetheart. 'The One'.

Back then my mum was working as a barmaid at a pub called The Cabbage Patch in Twickenham. She'd not been in London long. She grew up in Ireland and was the eighth of fifteen children born to Tommy and Winnie Maughan. The Maughans were a traveller family. Mum was born in County Mayo but her early childhood was spent moving between traveller camps all over the Republic of and Northern Ireland, from Dublin to Belfast and back again, while her father looked for whatever work he could get.

The traveller life is often romanticized but there was nothing lovely about my mother's childhood. Her memories are of a poverty-stricken existence, where getting enough to eat was never a given, punctuated by my grandfather's violent outbursts. The Maughan children often went hungry and they were always covered in bruises. Sometimes even burn marks. My grandfather would heat the back of a spoon over the campfire and use it to brand his terrified kids like they were animals. Mum still flinches when she talks about it. You never forget the feeling of hot metal on skin.

When Mum was nine and the family moved to Dublin, those burn marks brought her and her younger siblings to the attention of social services who feared, quite rightly, that it was only a matter of time before Tommy Maughan actually killed one of his kids. Mum's talked about the secret relief she felt when it was decided that she and the little ones should be taken away from Tommy and Winnie and placed in a children's home. They were going to be safe at last.

The Sisters of Nazareth home must have seemed like a taste of heaven at first. After years of scrabbling to find enough food, Mum and the little ones were suddenly getting three proper meals a day. Their filthy clothes were replaced with nice clean sets. There was running water. It was usually warm. But it wasn't long before it turned out that the nuns looking after the Maughan children were far from angels of mercy. It was a case of out of the frying pan . . .

The scandal of the children's homes run by the Catholic Church in Ireland is well documented now. Mum's experience, and that of her siblings, is depressingly familiar. The regime in the home was harsh and unfair. The smallest examples of misbehaviour were met with enthusiastic physical punishment from the nuns and priests. Meanwhile, local paedophiles, pretending to be 'volunteers', had free access to the children at all hours. The abuse the children suffered in those homes was in many cases far worse than the deprivation from which they had supposedly been rescued. The legacy of that abuse, of which more later, is only just beginning to be understood.

At the age of sixteen, Mum couldn't wait to get away from the Sisters of Nazareth at last. And it sounds sweet to hear that on the morning of her birthday her parents were waiting for her at the doors of the home. But Tommy and Winnie weren't there to welcome her back into the fold; they were there to tell her they'd arranged her marriage to the son of a rival traveller family. Arranged marriage was common in the traveller community as a way of ending feuds and cementing alliances, but to Mum the idea of going from a brutal children's home to what would inevitably be an unhappy union with a man she didn't even really know, let alone love, was understandably unappealing. She shook her parents off for long enough to make a real escape. She'd been given a little money upon leaving the home and it was just enough to buy a ferry ticket to the UK. She left Ireland for London the following day.

When I think about Mum at this point in her life, I have to admire her bravery. She didn't know anyone in England and even in the late 1970s it was still common to see signs saying 'no dogs, no blacks, no Irish' on the doors of London's B & Bs. But Mum managed to find a place to live, got a job as a barmaid and worked hard to support herself. Maybe, compared to the harshness of her upbringing, London didn't seem so unfriendly after all. Mum certainly had her admirers at The Cabbage Patch pub.

Most determined of those was my dad, Kevin Michael Wright. Mum's Mr Wright, as she thought of him then.

My dad was good-looking. He was charming. And he offered

Mum something she'd never had before – protection. He told her he wanted to look after her. After all those years of trying to look after herself and her younger siblings, when she should have been able to depend on her parents and the nuns, it's no wonder Mum fell in love with Dad's promises.

On the surface, Dad's background looks very different from Mum's. Mum's Irish traveller family was staunchly Catholic – something which would later cause friction. Meanwhile Dad came from three generations of Protestant Londoners. His grandfather and great-grandfather before him were fishmongers from Kingston upon Thames. Dad's father, William 'Bill' Wright, fought in the Second World War. Bill's wife Beryl was a great beauty. Together they had six children: five daughters and my dad. From the outside, they were a respectable working-class family. There was no way the Wright daughters or my dad would end up in care like the Maughan children had.

But the respectable facade was just that. There were skeletons in the Wright family cupboard to rival anything the Maughans had to hide. There had been no idyllic family upbringing for my grandfather Bill Wright. He'd in fact grown up in a series of children's homes. His own parents were divorced – a serious embarrassment in the 1920s – and Bill had had to carry that stigma. It could also be that my grandfather experienced more horror during wartime than he ever let on as he saw active service. Perhaps that was why he became a hard drinker, prone to violent outbursts just like my grandfather on Mum's side. As a child, Dad could only watch and cower.

There are plenty of studies that suggest we end up falling in love with people who fit the way of living we learned as small children. If we had an unhappy or abusive childhood, we may think we're choosing the opposite when we look for a partner but somehow the familiar patterns always re-emerge. If Dad started out wanting to protect my mum, it wasn't long before he became the one she needed to be protected *from*.

In 1982, however, Dad and Mum were still love's young dream. Though Dad didn't even have a job, they got married five days after Valentine's Day at Hounslow Register Office. They made a beautiful couple – Mum with her long dark locks and Dad with his long blond hair.

Dad had been over the moon when Mum got pregnant and vowed he would take care of her and the baby she was carrying until the day he died. But marriage and parenthood weren't as easy as they'd hoped. How could it be, when neither had ever really seen how successful families work? Neither of them ever had anything like proper role models. They'd grown up thinking that unhappiness was dealt with by drinking it away. Arguments were settled with a slap.

The argument that finally broke Mum and Dad apart was over religion and me.

I was still a baby when it happened. Mum wanted me to be christened a Catholic. Dad wasn't having it. He knew how the nuns had treated her. What kind of Christianity was that? Why would she want to have anything to do with the church that set her up to suffer so much? But, like a dog who loves a brutal owner, the treatment Mum endured in Ireland had not broken her trust in God. She couldn't shake off her devotion to the Catholic Church. Together with one of her friends from the children's home, Mum took me to Luton to be christened in secret.

As I later heard the story from my aunts and uncles, when Mum let Dad know what she'd done the resulting row went nuclear. Dad was furious that Mum had gone behind his back and done the one thing he didn't want her to do. He resorted to using his fists to win the point.

Dad's rage was out of all proportion to what poor Mum had done. Suddenly terrified of the man she once saw as her knight in shining armour, Mum fled, taking me with her.

From then on, my early years are a blur. I know from what Mum's told me since that we were always on the move, changing addresses every couple of weeks to stay one step ahead of my father. We moved from School Road in Hounslow to a women's refuge in Old Isleworth. Then we decamped to the Green Dragon Estate in Brentford before settling for a while in another women's refuge in Kew. We were proper fugitives, relying on kindness and charity. However, looking back, it wasn't always as though Mum didn't want us to be found. Though we were meant to be in hiding, Dad seemed to track us down quite easily.

When Dad turned up he would be bearing flowers and presents and promising that things would be different, and time after time Mum was convinced. Theirs was a crazy love. Maybe the making up made the breaking up seem worth it. It must have felt natural to them. After all, they'd both grown up in families where violence was seen as a legitimate means of communication. No matter what you'd done, no matter how bad it got, it was all right if you said 'sorry' afterwards. That was certainly what Dad seemed to think. That's what counted. If you did your best to make up, the other person had to forgive you. He loved my mum. His outbursts were proof of his passion. She'd *made* him feel that way. He'd never actually kill her. They were meant to be together, he'd tell her. Mum fell for it every time, throwing herself back into his arms.

On one of those occasions, when Mum and Dad got back together for a while, Mum became pregnant with my younger sister, Maria. Once again, Dad had a chance to prove that he could shape up and be the husband and protector he'd promised to be.

I don't have many clear memories from when I was small but I do have a memory of this brief time when they were reconciled. I must have been about two. I'm with both my parents. We're in a field somewhere. It must have been Richmond Park; they sometimes took me there. It's summer. The sun is shining and we're sitting on a blanket surrounded by tall grass. We've been having a picnic. It feels good to be with both of them, seeing them so happy. Happy to be with each other. Happy to have me with them. Mum is beautiful and kind and Dad is handsome and funny. They're both so young. They love each other and they both love me. In that perfect sun-kissed moment, I'm the luckiest kid in the world.

By the time Maria was born, however, me and Mum were already on the run again, back moving from hostel to hostel. Meanwhile Dad was sinking into addiction. He'd blown his chance to be a good dad and husband. The fairy tale was well and truly done.

After several months in the women's refuge, we finally had a home of our own. The council found Mum a flat on the Ivybridge Estate in Isleworth.

It sounds pretty but the Ivybridge Estate was not a great place to live. It was dominated by four big white tower blocks, built in the 1970s, and, to be blunt, the place stank of shit. The estate was right next door to the sewage plant that processed all of Hounslow's crap. There was no point stepping outside your front door for a breath of fresh air. The Ivybridge residents should have been supplied with gas masks.

That said, while we may have been living in a literal shithole, the Ivybridge was a fantastic place to be a kid. We didn't have much compared to the rest of London but we had each other. Everyone was broke. Everyone was battling demons like addiction, poverty or family breakdown. Everyone understood that life was hard. As a result there was a mad sense of community spirit. Everyone looked out for everyone else.

Living on the Ivybridge was definitely better than living in a hostel with so many other fearful people, waiting for the next angry bloke to turn up and start demanding to see his kids and threatening murder to anyone who tried to stop him. I might miss having other playmates around 24/7, but I wouldn't miss the tears and the shouting, the continuously being on alert. It was just us again. Me, Mum and Maria. Dad didn't know where we were. Everything was going to be fine. We didn't need to run anymore.

Mum soon felt settled enough on the Ivybridge Estate to invite two of her younger sisters, Bridget and Kathleen, over from Ireland to join us. They were old enough to leave the children's home by now and, like Mum, they were determined they weren't going back to their parents on the traveller camp. Never again.

I was about three years old then and delighted to have the

company of my two young aunts. They filled the two-bed first-floor flat with noise and laughter. Bridget and Kathleen knew how to have fun. They were always ready with a joke or a story. There was always music and dancing when my aunts were around. They were big fans of Madonna and UB40. I liked to dance about for them, making them roar with mirth at my antics, doing the actions to 'Rat in Mi Kitchen' and 'Red Red Wine'. I was a natural entertainer. I loved to make them laugh.

But all the partying had a dark side. Mum had always liked a drink. With her sisters around, she started drinking more than ever. The three of them would stay up late into the night, talking about life back in Ireland and what had happened in the children's home, and before then when they were still with their parents in the traveller camps. Bridget and Kathleen looked quite different to Mum. They were both taller and paler than she was, which had given rise over the years to suspicions that Mum might have a different dad. As a result, she'd always taken the worst of the beatings from their father.

Maybe drinking was the only thing that made those painful conversations bearable. Whatever, night after night they got smashed on booze bought with the money that was meant to buy food for my little sister and me. In the mornings they would all be too hung-over to get us kids ready for the day, complaining if we tried to wake them up too early.

I didn't mind. Back then I didn't know any different. While my mum and her sisters slept off the alcohol, I was happy to amuse myself. And, like most kids, I loved being able to play with the things that should have been off limits. No one was around to tell me not to.

It was on one of those mornings that the accident happened.

Mum, her sisters and their mates had been up partying until the early hours of the morning. They were all asleep, piled on Mum's bed. I was getting bored waiting for someone to wake up and give me some breakfast so I got out of bed and wandered into the kitchen on my own. I was a big boy. That's what they were always telling me when they were awake and I wanted some help. I was going to sort out breakfast for myself.

The kitchen was a mess. The table was covered in empty beer cans and bottles from the night before. There were others on the floor, left where they had fallen or been dropped. Dozens of cigarettes had been stubbed out on dirty plates. I picked a dog-end up and tried putting it to my mouth like the adults did. It made me gag. I took a swig from a half-finished can of beer to get rid of the lingering taste. I didn't like that much either. I needed some food. Someone had made themselves a late-night snack of cold baked beans. The empty tin was on the kitchen counter. The tin opener was on the mat by the door.

It wasn't exactly the latest 'must have' toy but the tin opener was fascinating to three-year-old me. I'd seen my mother and her sisters using it, of course. It was part of the mysterious adult world, like the knives I was always being warned to keep away from.

'Don't touch anything in this drawer,' the grown-ups used to say. 'You'll have your hand off.'

But the tin-opener wasn't in the drawer and it wasn't as dangerous as a knife, right? I sat down on the kitchen tiles and picked it up, determined to work it out for myself.

I wasn't yet dressed. I didn't have any pyjamas, or certainly not any clean ones. Sitting on the dirty tiles, I turned the tin-opener over and over. It seemed gigantic to me. I had to use two hands to hold it. I squeezed the handles together and tried to twist the crank. The tin-opener was old and half-rusted up. Making it turn was hard but I was fascinated. Though I was naked and the tiles were cold, I was completely absorbed in getting it to work. I got an empty can and turned it over. I decided I'd try to take the bottom of the can off.

Had I been wearing any clothes, it might have made a difference to what happened next. Because somehow I managed to use it to cut open my testicles.

The pain was instantaneous and unbearable. I screamed the place down. If my mum and her sisters had been sleeping off their hangovers, they weren't sleeping anymore.

I don't remember how I got to the hospital that day. I think I passed out. I assume Mum must have carried me. After seeing the blood and waking the house with my screams, I blacked out. The horror of what happened made me blank the details of the hospital visit that followed for years to come. But it did happen – I've got the scars – and, in a way that shocks me now, it became something of a family joke, with my mother and my aunts retelling the story as though it was a comedy sketch. A three-year-old. Left alone in the kitchen without supervision in a house full of adults too drunk to take proper care of the kids. Cutting open his own balls with a tin opener. Yeah. Fucking hilarious. Over thirty years later, I still can't laugh about it.

I recently tried to find the medical records relating to the accident but discovered that all my records from birth until the age of twelve were missing. Naturally, because of my father's history of violence and addiction and the fact that we'd gone through several women's shelters, my sister and I were already

17

on the radar of social services. Later, a solicitor told me that we were on the 'at risk' register. Discovering that my medical records were missing, I wonder if social services were even aware of the accident. Maybe the missing records were the result of an administrative error. Maybe not. Were strings pulled to make sure nobody knew what had happened so I could stay in that flat with Mum and her sisters?

Up until then, I'd known nothing other than the life I lived. Though I was too young to make much sense of events, there was no doubt that in my world it was normal to see your father yelling in your mother's face. It was normal to go on the run and stay in a hostel full of other women and children living in fear for their lives. It was normal for the adults in my family to get wasted while the kids were left to fend for themselves.

But now I began to distrust pretty much all the adults in my life. And I somehow knew instinctively that what Uncle Tommy wanted me to do was wrong.

2

Tommy Maughan Junior was Mum's youngest brother. He was just two years old when he was taken from the traveller camp into the care of the Sisters of Nazareth and, by all accounts, of all the Maughan children he had the worst time of it. At the very least, he was in the children's home the longest. But it's likely that he was both physically and sexually abused by the priests and their paedophile friends who visited the home. Thinking about Tommy's childhood, separated from his siblings and surrounded by so many predators, there was little chance he would grow into anything other than a dysfunctional adult himself.

I was still a little kid, almost four, when Tommy came to stay. It wasn't long after the tin-opener incident. Tommy was in his late teens when he turned up at our flat with everything he owned, which wasn't much. He'd left the Catholic children's home at sixteen, just as his siblings had done before him, and spent a few years knocking around in Belfast, trying to make a life for himself. Then he came to London looking for work.

I don't know if I looked forward to having an uncle in the house. I was already a bit distrustful of men, having experienced my dad's violent rages. In the women's hostels, any male over the age of ten was viewed with suspicion, and I'd taken that on board. My sister Maria and I had learned that men were angry, violent and cruel. But Mum couldn't turn her brother away, could she? Not after helping her little sisters as best she could. Mum's parents might have let the Maughan children down but she wasn't going to. It was only right that Tommy moved in now.

I can picture him clearly, sitting on the battered sofa in his donkey jacket, rolling one of his thin cigarettes. He was a big guy – maybe six feet two – but he was pale-skinned with a baby face that gave him an innocent look for his age. I watched him shyly from the other side of the room, mesmerized by his long fingers and the way they moved as he went about his delicate task. Tommy entertained us with stories about his life back in Ireland, about the trouble he and his mates got themselves into, how they lived the wild life and flouted the law. Though they claimed benefits, they made money by tarmacking driveways and collecting scrap. It was all cash in hand. They were always hustling. It was the gypsy way. When they had money, they partied hard. The Maughan men had an air of glamour to them the way Tommy told it. They were like cowboys or pirates or highwaymen to me.

Like Mum and his sisters, Tommy liked a drink. And when he was drinking, he liked to listen to an Irish band called The Wolfe Tones. They were a long way from my aunts' favourite Madonna. The Wolfe Tones were named after an eighteenth-century Irish rebel called Theobald Wolfe Tone, their songs were based on traditional music and their lyrics were all about the Troubles. One of Tommy's favourite songs was 'Rifles of the I.R.A.', with its lyrics about not yet being free but not forgetting.

There was something about Tommy that put me on edge immediately. I didn't know what the Troubles were. I had no idea what Tommy had lived through in the children's home. All I knew was that Tommy seemed to be unpredictable. Like The Wolfe Tones' music he loved so much, Tommy was full of suppressed anger that seemed ready to explode at any time. But he was my uncle and as his nephew I had to submit to his cuddles and the rough-housing he insisted on. He was Mum's little brother. She loved him like I loved my little sister, Maria, she explained. I had to love Uncle Tommy too. He was family. End of.

It started soon after he moved in.

Michael the happy toddler playing in the long grass between his doting parents was long gone. At almost four, I saw the world very differently. Though I'd never really known him, I missed Dad and sometimes that made me angry. When I got angry, I kicked off. When I kicked off, Mum would pick me up and shut me in the bedroom until I calmed down. That's what she always did. Until now. Casting himself as the man of the house in the absence of any other, Tommy, Mum's loving brother, my doting uncle, volunteered to try to make me see where I was going wrong. Mum thought it was a good idea. He could talk to me 'man to man' and be the role model I didn't have now Dad was gone.

One evening I had a tantrum about not wanting to eat my tea, or something trivial like that. Once again, I pushed it too far so Mum shut me in the bedroom as she usually did. I didn't care. I was used to that. I could take it. I just had to wait it out. However, ten minutes later Tommy came in just to see how I was 'getting on'.

I looked up at my uncle, surprised and a little bit anxious to see him there instead of Mum. He stepped into the room and closed the door behind him. He kneeled down and made me get out of bed and stand in front of him, like a kid in front of the headmaster.

'Now what do you think you're doing, upsetting your mother like that?'

Tommy gave me a lecture. That was bad enough. But at some point during the conversation about my bad behaviour, he reached out and grabbed me by the balls. I must have cried out or even screamed but no one came to help me. I don't know whether Tommy knew it was a particularly terrible thing to do to me, after the accident, but it seems likely that he did. My mum and aunts used the accident as part of the family comedy routine after all. It's unlikely that they hadn't told Tommy about it.

As Tommy held my testicles, the pain made me feel like my soul was squeezing out of my body. I thought I was going to pass out. However, it wasn't the worst thing. Anger, I was used to. Pain, I could take. But Uncle Tommy wanted something else.

At first, Tommy only came into the bedroom when Mum sent him in to talk to me, but it wasn't long before he began to visit in the middle of the night when everyone else was asleep. Maria slept in a cot in Mum's room, so I was alone. Tommy was meant to sleep on the sofa but I would wake to find him standing next to my bed, looking down at me like he was some kind of ghost. I'd try to scramble upright.

'Shh,' he'd say, putting a finger on my lips and pushing me back down into the pillows. 'We don't want to wake everyone else up now, do we, Mikey?' Mikey was what he always called me.

Then he'd make me budge up and lie down on the bed beside me, spooning me as though we were lovers, his hands creeping round to the front of my young boy's body, sliding across my bare skin. He'd touch my genitals. I could do nothing but keep as still as possible, hoping he would go away as soon as he got what he wanted. That's what usually happened. He'd stroke my body until I heard him make some weird sort of sigh then he'd get up and go away again without a word. After he'd gone, I'd lie awake, too frightened and confused even to cry.

I was too young to know what was really going on but I began to dread the sound of The Wolfe Tones, which told me that Tommy was drinking and would soon be on his way to my room again.

Later, Tommy got braver. Like lots of kids, I made dens around the house by draping sheets and blankets over the furniture, creating my own little world underneath. I would make dens under the kitchen table – perhaps to be close to Mum while she was cooking or cleaning – but I wasn't safe even there. Tommy would climb in with me, touching me where he shouldn't while my mother was standing just feet away. It wasn't just the nights that held fear for me now. It would happen in the middle of the day. Just a blanket hiding what he was doing from the other adults in the house. Tommy didn't care. I was terrified but he knew I would not breathe a word. Tommy had me so convinced that if I said anything about him, it would be me and only me who suffered.

It's the smell that lingers in my memory still. The dirty

tobacco smell of his fingers when he put his hand across my mouth to stop me crying out as he climbed into bed beside me. Those fingers stinking and yellow from those skinny little roll-ups that he made with such care. Then the taste when he put his fingers actually in my mouth, making me gag. The stale alcohol on his breath as he panted over my shoulder. I wanted to bite him but I didn't have the guts. I was a kid. He was a grown man. He could have killed me with his bare hands. That's what I thought was the truth.

'Don't tell anyone,' he said. 'If you tell, no one will believe you anyway.'

I was terrified of my Uncle Tommy. When he told me that he would kill me if anyone found out what was going on, I believed it. He'd told me enough stories about the hard men he knew back in Northern Ireland. Real-life members of the IRA. Bogeymen in balaclavas. Tommy was their friend. He could have me sorted out in the middle of the night and no one would know who had done it. No one would ask questions. No one would care.

I was trapped. I couldn't tell Mum what was going on. As far as she was concerned, Uncle Tommy was the apple of her eye. He was her little brother. She knew what he'd been through at the children's home and she wanted him to be happy with her. Irrational as it was, Mum felt guilty for everything her younger siblings had been through. Having been unable to protect Tommy as a child, she wanted to do her best for him now.

For Mum, family life was about making things better again. Ironically, by opening our home to the younger siblings she felt so responsible for, Mum invited hell into my life and that of my sister. The Maughan children had finally left the children's home and half of them were safe in our happy flat in London. That's what Mum thought. But they brought with them the ugly ghosts of the abuse they had suffered. They handed their misery on as they drank to forget or re-enacted the abuse that had been meted out to them. Could they have done any differently? I don't know. All I knew was that my life was getting worse by the day.

Tommy's nocturnal visits continued the whole time he stayed with us. I wasn't safe anywhere. I tried to stick as close to Mum as I could but, not knowing what was really going on, she often left Tommy in charge while she went out to work. I didn't know how to escape.

What Tommy did to me left scars far worse than the accident with the tin-opener. I was guilty and confused. I knew what was going on was wrong but I was no longer sure who was at fault. Like many abusers, Tommy cleverly left me feeling as though I had somehow *invited* what happened by being naughty and upsetting my mum. I was the one who'd caused it. If anyone found out what he'd done to me, I was the one who would be in trouble. Not him.

I wonder now if that was how the priests who abused Tommy framed it too. Did they tell him *he'd* made them do it? *He* was the one who would have to answer to God. I knew from going to church with Mum that we were full of original sin. Maybe I deserved it.

I thought it would never end. However, six months or so after he arrived, Tommy left as suddenly as he had come. Mum tried to persuade him to stay but he told her he had to go back to Ireland. I didn't tell anyone how relieved I was to see him go, or why.

3

Maybe Uncle Tommy left our flat because he felt bad about what he'd been doing to me and wanted to get away from temptation. More likely he left because my mum was now in a serious relationship and her new bloke was around all the time. Mum had given up on Dad. We hadn't seen him in a couple of years, though apparently he was still living nearby. And still his old charismatic self, as I would discover decades later.

For now Mum's new boyfriend was far more reliable than Dad had ever been. Pete Maisey was smitten with Mum from their first blind date. She was beautiful and she was fun to be around. Pete treated her like a princess.

He made an impression on me from the start. He was a big man with a full beard. To me, a skinny five-year-old, he looked like a huge scary bear. Even when he was doing his best to make me and Maria warm to him because he loved our mum, Pete was intimidating.

When Mum invited Pete to move in, the dynamic of the flat changed again. No longer trying to make us like him, Pete morphed from being a friendly adult to a stepdad and he took his role seriously.

Apart from Tommy's early attempts, before he moved on to

other ways of scaring me, I'd never really experienced male discipline before. When I was in trouble with Pete, I was really in trouble. I can still remember the first time; he towered over me and shouted in my face until I cried. Long after he'd gone away again, I couldn't stop shaking. I wished I could ask Mum to tell him to go but, as with Tommy, she didn't see things from my point of view. She saw Pete as someone who would look after us all.

Pete was a good influence on Mum in some ways. Like all of Mum's friends, Pete drank, but he knew when to stop and that meant that when he was around Mum drank slightly less too. She didn't want to mess things up.

And Pete was determined that we should have an idyllic family life. He bought a caravan on Hayling Island and every school holiday we would decamp from Isleworth to stay there, just like a normal family.

Me and Maria loved Hayling Island. We'd never really had a proper holiday before. We loved the seaside and the novelty of camping. We quickly made friends with the other kids who were regulars, just as Mum and Pete had made friends with their parents. Jodie and Lee, who stayed in the caravan next door, were about the same age as me and Maria. We quickly formed a little gang. Our parents pretty much left us to our own devices on the campsite. We couldn't wander far and there was always a friendly adult nearby if we did get into trouble.

It was on Hayling Island that I had my own first experience of alcohol. I was with Jodie. She'd nicked a couple of cans from her parents' supply and we slipped off to a place where the adults wouldn't find us to drink it. It was Skol, a cheap brand of lager. Jodie opened the first can and took a sip, smacking her lips together like it was really delicious. She handed it to me next. I took a sip myself.

It was disgusting. The lager was warm and it tasted like wet wool. I hated it. But there was no question that I would have to drink some more so I pretended that I loved it. I passed the can back to Jodie and waited for the alcohol to take effect. What would it be like? Would I start laughing and singing like the adults did? Would I be able to walk when I stood up?

Some other kids joined us. It was a full moon that night. We could hear the adults laughing as they got pissed in someone's awning. They weren't worrying about us. The cans were passed round and round the circle. Soon all the kids we used to hang out with were there, daring each other to have more and more. I probably had about half a can in the end. Not much but enough to get an eight-year-old thoroughly drunk.

After I got over how bad the lager tasted, other feelings started to take over. As the alcohol did its work, I felt the world dissolve around me until there was only that moment, happy and safe with my friends, under the glowing moon. All the vague worries I'd been carrying around with me – about Mum, about Pete, about someone finding out about Tommy – just seemed to vanish. I was free. I felt good.

When I got back to the van no one noticed I'd been drinking. Mum was probably too drunk herself. I got into bed, still feeling like I was floating. It was as if I'd found a way out of the real world to go somewhere where everything would be all right.

There was plenty of opportunity to find stuff to drink that summer. We spent most of the school holidays in the van but Pete still had to work. He was a lorry driver, and during the week he would go back to Isleworth, leaving us alone with Mum. That's when she took a little break from reality of her own.

When Pete wasn't around, Mum felt free to party properly.

'This is my holiday too,' Mum would say as she left us alone in the van to go and meet her fellow drinkers.

There was one night when I wasn't happy about it. Pete had gone back to town that morning. As soon as he left, Mum opened a bottle of cheap Liebfraumilch and knocked back a generous glassful. I don't know why it felt different that day. I'd got used to her drinking and most of the time I was fine about it. Mum wasn't a mean drunk and her being out of it meant that I could get up to whatever I wanted with my mates. That day, though, I was feeling like I wanted her around. I wanted her to stay in the caravan with me and Maria that night. Keep us company for a change. Maybe it was because she'd been rowing with Pete over the weekend and I wanted her to stay off the booze so he wouldn't get angry again when he came back on Friday afternoon.

Mum shrugged off my request for her to stay with us. She told me that she wouldn't be long. She was just going to have one more drink with Sid and Joyce, who had a caravan a few pitches along from ours. Sid and Joyce were in their sixties. They were big into their drink and their caravan with its large awning was often the scene of spontaneous grown-up parties that went on into the small hours.

I begged Mum not to go over to Sid and Joyce's caravan that night. I tried telling her I didn't feel well. But Mum was determined. What kind of holiday was it for her if she had to sit in the van with us all night? She left me and Maria alone.

Resigned to the fact that Mum was going out again whether we liked it or not, we got ourselves ready for bed. We could hear Mum's laughter drifting in through the caravan windows. At least she was close by.

I don't know how much later it was that the door to the van flew open, banging loudly as it did so. I was startled awake to find a man looming over my bed. I was still half asleep as Sid grabbed me by the collar of my pyjamas and pulled me to my feet.

'Don't you ever try telling your mother what she can and can't do, you little shit,' he yelled into my face. He was shaking me like he was a dog and I was a rat. 'You little bastard. Don't you ever go cheeking your mother again.'

Sid ranted at me for what felt like forever. His whisky breath blasted in my face. I screwed my eyes shut then I started to cry and he shouted at me for that too.

'You're crying now, eh, crybaby. You're happy enough to have a go at your mother but you're not such a big boy now, eh?'

The tears streamed down my face. My legs were shaking. Still holding me by the collar, Sid lifted me so that my toes almost left the ground. I was a kid. He was a grown man, almost as big as Pete.

'You got that, sunshine? Don't you ever give your mother grief again.'

At last, Sid threw me back down onto the bed and crashed his way out of the caravan, leaving me and Maria alone once more. Mum came back hours later. She didn't mention my night-time visitor. I didn't dare complain.

*

What with Tommy, Pete and Sid, I was quickly learning that being in the company of men was not a safe place for me. At best, men were intimidating. They were frightening. They were violent. I didn't go back to sleep that night of Sid's visit, and forever afterwards I had trouble sleeping in the caravan.

It wasn't much better in Isleworth. Other kids had nightmares. I had my real dad.

It happened shortly after that summer. I was in bed in the flat on the Ivybridge Estate when I was woken by a commotion in the hall.

It was Dad. Kevin Wright. Drunk and high, he'd turned up at the flat determined to see me and my sister. Pete was blocking the door. Dad screamed that he had a right to see us but Pete told him to come back in the daytime, when he was sober. Dad was standing his ground.

I was terrified as I listened to the two men argue through a crack in the bedroom door. I was afraid that Dad might hurt Mum. I was afraid that Pete might hurt Dad. I was also afraid that Dad turning up might make Pete leave and, if Pete left but Dad wasn't back for good, then maybe Uncle Tommy would turn up again. I felt cold and shaky as I waited for the worst to happen.

Dad wasn't giving up and the shouting got louder. The way the flats were arranged on the Ivybridge Estate – facing in around the car park – meant that everyone soon knew everyone else's business and it wasn't long that night before one of our neighbours called the police to deal with the commotion that had by now woken everyone up.

The police car parked up in the middle of the estate with its blue light flashing off all the blocks. Faces peered down from every flat. Meanwhile, hardly daring to breathe, I listened as the police tried to reason with Dad on the doorstep. It took them a while to persuade him that it was a bad time to call on the kids he hadn't even seen in a couple of years. They escorted him away from the block. At last, Pete closed the door on the outside world again. When I dared to look out of the window, to see if I could catch a glimpse of my father, the police car and Dad were already gone. I got back into bed and pulled the covers up over my head. A few minutes later, Mum looked in. I pretended I was asleep.

I felt protected by Pete that night in Isleworth but in general our relationship was difficult. He had taken on a lot when he got together with my mother. Two kids. Her drinking. Her volatile ex. Pete wasn't yet a father himself. He'd gone from being a lad about town to a de facto stepdad in the space of a few months. There was no instruction manual. No wonder he found it hard to strike the right note when disciplining me and Maria.

The dynamic shifted again when my half-sister Sophie came along. I was ten at the time. Pete's attention – and Mum's – definitely moved to the new baby. It shifted again when my half-brother Justin came along. I believe that Pete cared for me and Maria but the love he had for his own biological kids was different. It was unconditional. Later on, seeing that unconditional love in action would make me realize what I didn't have in my life. A father who would love me no matter what. Someone who would do anything to help me succeed.

There were a couple of people who tried to offer me a glimpse of a different kind of future at that time.

Pete worked hard to support the family but Mum was also

working as a cleaner to help make ends meet. Isleworth was not a rich area by any means, but it wasn't far from some seriously wealthy parts of London, where one of Mum's clients was the Olympic athlete Sebastian Coe. Lord Coe, as he is now. When I was off sick from school one day, Mum had to take me along to Coe's house while she worked. I watched TV while she cleaned. It was a lovely house. Much bigger than the flat.

Coe came home while Mum and I were still there. Mum was nervous that he'd be upset that she'd brought one of her children to work, but Coe wasn't bothered at all. Instead, he went out of his way to try to get to know me. He asked me about school and about what I wanted to be when I grew up. He was kind and encouraging. He did his best and I wanted to like him but I was still wary. I knew how men could turn from friendly to violent in a heartbeat.

Then there was Mary.

Despite her horrific childhood in the Nazareth home, Mum was still devoted to the Catholic Church and every weekend she dragged me and Maria to Mass. I hated it. It was boring in the extreme. I'd just stare at the statues of Jesus and the saints and wait for it to be over. Those forty-five minutes every Sunday morning felt like a lifetime to me.

It was at the church that we met Mary, who lived in Percy Gardens, another Isleworth estate. She had a son the same age as my little brother Justin and that's how she connected with Mum. I liked Mary. She was very pretty, with long dark hair and green eyes, but more importantly, she was kind. She always took an interest in what was going on with me and my sister. She treated us like mini-adults and it was clear that she really cared.

I would have no idea how much she cared until years later. She was one of the few people who would never give up on me, despite everything that was to happen over the next ten years.

4

The first school I went to was a twenty-minute walk from our flat on the Ivybridge Estate. It was called St Mary's. Mum chose it because it was affiliated to the church.

I wasn't one of those kids who turned up at primary school already knowing how to read and write. Bedtime stories weren't ever part of the routine at home. Mum's dyslexic. Dad was never around. Though if he had been, it wouldn't have made a difference in terms of my education, given that he couldn't read or write.

So there were low expectations for my success at primary school, but when I put my mind to it I found I could do OK. The school arranged for me to have extra tuition, which helped a great deal. However, I had a serious problem with my short attention span. Now that I understand it better, I can see that I wasn't just being distracted, I was actually disassociating.

This is how it happened. I'd be in the classroom, trying to listen to what the teacher was telling us, when suddenly a thought about what had been going on outside school would start to intrude. I'd think about Dad smacking Mum around. Or Sid waking me up to scream in my face. I'd think about Tommy touching me in a way I didn't want to be touched. The only way I could deal with it was to let my mind go completely blank. It was the only way I could feel safe.

'Michael! Michael!' The teachers tried to regain my attention, but after a while most of them gave up. They didn't know what was going through my mind. They put it down to my being thick.

There were good moments, though. There were teachers who guessed and understood that my home life wasn't great, like Mrs Ridley.

Mrs Ridley probably had no idea how she would change my perspective when she cast me in a play called *Mr Macaroni and the Exploding Pizza Pie* when I was ten years old.

It was a major part. I had to learn a lot of lines, which wasn't easy, but it was a transformative experience. Quite literally. The character of Wordsworth had his own set of feelings, but when I was in character his feelings became mine. Though he was fictional, Wordsworth's thoughts crowded my own bad thoughts out. The sensation of stepping out onto the stage was like the first time I tried alcohol. I felt as though I was floating once more. As long as I was pretending to be someone else, I was free of myself.

I was ecstatic when we finished the first performance. The applause lifted me to a place where, even if only for a moment, I could be absolutely happy. I was crushed when the last performance ended, wondering how I would get to feel that again. So when Mrs Ridley asked me to be in another play I jumped at the chance.

There was clearly something in acting for me. Shortly after my debut as Wordsworth I got a walk-on part in the BBC sitcom *Birds of a Feather*, thanks to Mrs Ridley's connections. It was a big deal. *Birds of a Feather* was huge at the time. Everyone I knew watched the show and loved it. I was incredibly excited to get a part, no matter how tiny.

In the show, Pauline Quirke's character, Sharon, had a nephew who was about my age. The episode I appeared in was about that nephew taking part in a football tournament. I was going to play one of his teammates.

It was a small part. I didn't even have any lines but Pauline Quirke in particular treated me like a star. Because we were recording some of the scenes outside, during the lunch break the cast and crew all ate together on a double-decker bus that had been converted into a mobile canteen. Pauline invited me to join her. When I got onto the bus I couldn't believe the sight that greeted me. There was an enormous buffet loaded with all my favourite foods. I didn't know where to start.

'You can have whatever you want,' Pauline told me. My eyes bugged open and she laughed to see me so excited. This kind of spread was perfectly normal for a film set. I sat with her to eat lunch that day. She was really kind and warm and I soon felt comfortable chatting with her. She asked me if I'd thought about acting as a career. She said, 'Because I think you could do well.' What I heard when she said that was, 'I believe in you.' I had never heard that before in my life and it gave me a real boost. It gave me hope. Maybe I was capable of something good.

After *Birds of a Feather*, I really had the acting bug. I auditioned for a show called *The Biz* and had a set of headshots done. I was ready to be a star. But my career as a child actor was to be short-lived. I was still a kid. I couldn't go to auditions or work on screen or stage without a chaperone. But Mum's alcoholism was getting worse. Combining that with looking after my little half-siblings meant she just didn't have time to ferry me around like other parents did. Pete was too busy working. So I missed out on those early opportunities that came my way and my dream slipped out of reach.

I tried to pretend that it never really mattered to me anyway. I told myself I'd been stupid to even think I could do well at something so special.

Things were getting worse at home for other reasons. When Pete came into our lives, Maria and I were still really young. We started calling him 'Dad' soon after he moved in. Meanwhile Mum tore up all her photos of our real dad. We didn't see him. Mum didn't talk about him. That was why I'd been so frightened when he turned up that night at the flat. Kevin Wright was pretty much a stranger to me.

By the time I was ten, though, I started to wonder about him again. I knew Pete was different with my half-siblings, his biological children. There was no doubt about that. I seemed to wind him up without even trying. He had more patience for them. They had his unconditional love. Me and Maria couldn't count on that.

Though Mum didn't ever hold back in telling me and Maria what a low-life Kevin Wright was, when things were difficult at home with Pete I started to think that maybe my real dad could save me. He could come back into my life and take me away to live with him. I wouldn't have to watch Mum get drunk or have Pete yelling in my face or lie in bed in the caravan fearing that one of Mum's mates was going to come in and attack me. My real dad would take me away from all that. He would be my real live hero.

The reality was very different.

A couple of years had passed since the night Dad turned up at the Ivybridge Estate and the police had to be called to calm him down and get him to leave us alone. And leave us alone he did. Not only did he not come back to the flat again, he didn't bother to call to find out how we were. He didn't even send a birthday or Christmas card. I'd got used to not hearing from him.

I don't know if Mum knew where he was throughout all those years. It seems unlikely that she would have lost tabs on him altogether. They'd been so deeply in love, it would have been hard for her to stop caring. But now she had Pete and there was no doubt that he didn't want her to be in touch with her ex, so Mum never arranged for us to see him. But he hadn't gone far and it was inevitable that one day he'd pop up again.

It was summer. I was nearly eleven. We'd been to the shops, just Mum, Maria and me. We were heading back home along Feltham High Street when Mum suddenly exclaimed, 'There's your dad.'

I looked out of the window, expecting to see Pete. At first I didn't recognize the man she was pointing out to me and my sister. In my mind, my real dad was as he had been that day in Richmond Park. Mum was pointing at a much older man, who was shuffling along with his head down as though he was in a hurry to get somewhere without being seen on the way. He was skinny, weak and pale. He was drinking from a can of Holsten Pils. I've never forgotten that yellow can.

'Do you want to talk to him?' Mum asked.

I wasn't sure. For so long I'd been imagining what it would be like to talk to my dad. I'd imagined telling him all my worries and having him take their weight. The man shuffling along in a dirty coat didn't look like the kind of man who'd understand. But Mum was already pulling the car up alongside the kerb. She unbuckled her seatbelt and got out of the car. Maria and I followed her.

'Kevin!' she shouted after him. He turned round, looking furtive, like someone who had reason to be nervous when people called his name on the street. 'Kevin!'

When Dad realized that it was Mum who was calling him, his face changed. He straightened up a bit. He flashed her a smile, like the smiles she must have fallen in love with. He walked back to where we were standing and looked at me and Maria as though he wasn't sure who we were. When it clicked, he ruffled my hair, as though I was a nephew or a friend's kid, not his own flesh and blood. Not his son.

'Fancy seeing you here,' he said.

We walked with Dad to the duck pond. It was no great family moment. Dad asked how we were – me and Maria – but he didn't seem that bothered to hear our answers. In retrospect, I can see that Dad was more interested in Mum than in me or Maria. He probably thought he had a chance of getting his leg over. Whatever, it was pretty clear that Maria and I came way down his list of priorities, and when he worked out that he wasn't going to get his leg over he started to lose interest in talking to Mum as well. After only about half an hour, he said he had somewhere he needed to be. Looking back, I think he must have been on his way to score some drugs. When we parted, he hurried off. He didn't look back or wave.

I was silent on the drive home.

After that meeting, I felt real sadness and disappointment.

I had invested everything in Dad coming into my life like some fatherly version of a knight in shining armour. Meeting him in reality had left me with nothing. Worse than nothing. Looking back now, I can see that because of my fantasy I'd refused to let Pete get close to me. It seemed like it would be a betrayal of Dad. What a joke. While I had been dreaming that he was going to make everything better, Dad wasn't thinking about me at all. My own father wasn't interested in me. I'd pushed Pete away. I had nothing. I was nothing.

It wasn't long after that things took a real turn for the worse. Maria and I came home from school one day to find that Mum wasn't there. Pete met us at the door looking upset and anxious. Mum was in hospital. She'd had a heart attack.

To a kid still at primary school, the words 'heart attack' were terrifying. It was one of the ways people died without warning. That's all I knew. I'd heard people talking about it in church, after one of the older members of the congregation died suddenly. I didn't think anybody survived one.

Pete loaded us into the car and drove us to see Mum, while one of the neighbours looked after the little ones. Mum was sitting up in bed but she was pale and looked exhausted. Seeing her like that stunned me into silence. I'd never visited anyone in hospital except when Mum had my younger brother and sister. Those were happy visits. The atmosphere around Mum's bed now was very different.

'You've got to be good for Pete,' Mum told me. 'He can't put up with any nonsense now.'

Pete was working – he had recently bought a burger van from his father John – and now he was in sole charge of four kids. Thankfully, Mum's sisters pitched up and helped out as soon as they could. I was worried about being left alone with Pete because I knew that Mum's heart attack was my fault. I was convinced of it. With childish logic, I drew a direct line between the way I'd been behaving at school – badly – with Mum getting so stressed her heart gave out. She'd told me several times that she couldn't take the stress of me misbehaving. I thought it was a matter of time before Pete made the connection too. I didn't know or understand that Mum had a congenital heart condition that was exacerbated by her heavy drinking and smoking.

Mum didn't disabuse me of the idea that it was all my fault. In fact, when she had a second heart attack six months later, she picked up on how guilty I was feeling and used it as leverage, telling me that if I didn't behave at school it would kill her.

As I got older and I started to understand how my life was different from that of my mates, I was finding it harder and harder to control my temper at school. The other kids, sensing my weakness, took advantage of the fact. The tiniest thing could set me off. One of my classmates' favourite jokes was to call me 'Michael Left' or 'Michael Wrong' instead of Michael Wright. It was a little thing. A stupid thing. Not even remotely funny or clever. But it got me every time. I hated being called Michael Left and anyone who dared utter those words had to be taught a lesson. I spent a lot of time chasing kids down for this insult.

Maybe, subconsciously, the reason it got to me so badly was because to me, when those kids were calling me 'Michael Left' it wasn't just a pun on left and right. The fact was, I *had* been left. My dad, the original Michael Wright, the man who gave me my name in the first place, had walked out and walked away. I never heard from him. I didn't even know where he was. And, of course, because I didn't understand any better, because as a child I knew nothing about the forces of addiction and how they tear families apart, I framed his absence in the way kids do. I made it all about *me*. I decided he must have left because of something *I* did. He left because he didn't love *me* anymore. I was a bad son. A terrible child who deserved to be abandoned and left to the mercies of people like my Uncle Tommy. If my own father didn't want me, it had to be because I wasn't good enough. I made people leave.

Michael *Left* was exactly who I feared I had become. Michael *Wrong* was who I was.

Fortunately for me, or rather for my classmates, that was about to change.

Mum and Pete Maisey had been together for a long time by now, yet Mum had kept Pete at arm's length, refusing to make their relationship official, as though subconsciously she was still waiting for Dad to clean up his act and come home. Everyone else could see that wasn't ever going to happen. And now Pete was getting impatient. He gave Mum that ultimatum. It was time she married him.

Maria and I found out how Mum had responded to the ultimatum when we got home from school one very ordinary afternoon. Mum and Pete sat me and my sister down at the kitchen table and announced they'd got married at the registry office that morning. They were Mr and Mrs Maisey. Job done. That was how we learned that Pete was now officially our new dad.

A wedding is usually a cause for celebration but I didn't know what to think that afternoon. At the weddings I'd heard about, children were a big part of the occasion. My sister could have been a bridesmaid. I could have worn a little suit and carried the rings. There should have been a big party with dancing and cake. Why hadn't they asked us to join in? Why didn't they even tell us until afterwards? Though only the youngest of us – Justin – had actually been at the wedding, because he was the only one of us who didn't have school, I decided that Mum had left me out because I didn't matter. Me and Maria weren't really a proper part of the new family she and Pete had created. My half-siblings mattered more to Pete than we did. Mum and Pete wanted me to be happy for them but I was devastated. I didn't feel part of this new family and now I knew for sure I would never have my old family back either.

Mum's finally marrying Pete firmly shut the door on any fantasy I might have had of going back to that sunny day in Richmond Park. Me – and Maria this time – together with Mummy and Daddy. Together and happy and looking forward to better days ahead. As a family. That was never going to happen again. I no longer even shared my real dad's name. I was Michael Maisey now.

5

Mum wanted me to go to St Mark's, a Catholic school, when I left my primary. I didn't get in. My academic and behaviour records weren't good enough. However, after Mum had her two heart attacks she persuaded her priest to write to the school on our behalf, pleading our case and explaining all the trouble our family had recently gone through due to Mum's ill health. It worked. I got my place at St Mark's.

Mum was delighted – she hoped that going to St Mark's would straighten me out – but I wasn't convinced. Though some of my mates would be going to St Mark's with me, my best mate was going to Gunnersbury. That St Mark's was so far away from where we lived was a huge downside too. The journey involved two buses, and a change at the Hounslow Bus Garage. That was where kids from all the local schools would gather every morning and evening. Among the pupils from Hounslow Manor and Lampton schools – both of which were best described as rough – a kid on his way to St Mark's really stood out.

The first year was hell. I was a sweet little eleven-year-old wearing a blazer. Every journey to school was like running through the middle of a battlefield. I was jeered at, spat at and tripped up by the Hounslow Manor and Lampton boys. And it wasn't much better in school. I was trying to keep up my end of the bargain I'd made with Mum – that I'd stay out of trouble so she didn't have another heart attack – I worked hard and did my best to keep my head down, but that didn't help me with the cool kids. They were provoked by what they saw as my swottiness and also by the fact that I was starting to get attention from some of the girls. I didn't court it; it just happened. I was too shy to know how to respond. They thought I looked cute. That did me no favours with the boys who were interested in girls but couldn't get a look-in. They started calling me 'pretty boy' and took to tripping me up or pushing me over in front of the girls to humiliate me. They always seemed to do it when I had something in my hands so I couldn't save myself and would end up flat on my nose, surrounded by a crowd of jeering faces.

I began to dread every school day. A day of taunts and bullying sandwiched between two journeys through no-man's land. Still, I did my best not to let Mum down. I didn't feel like I could tell her what it was really like to be at St Mark's. It seemed to make her happy to see me go off in my blazer every day. If she saw me, that is. If she wasn't sleeping off a heavy night.

It was towards the end of year seven that the crunch came. It was a Friday. The kids in my class who'd been making my life difficult all summer term let it be known that I was in for it that day. I heard the whispers. I didn't know what to do. Should I stay in the library or leg it, getting out of school as soon as I could when the bell rang, hoping that I'd be long gone before my tormentors were ready to come after me? I spent the whole day in a state of anxiety, imagining the beating I was going to get that afternoon.

In the end, I decided against the library. They'd only wait for me to come out. They had nothing else to do. I made the decision instead to try to brazen it out. I walked from the school gates as calmly as I could, though inside I was panicking like crazy. I tried to keep my head high but soon I had a whole gang of kids trailing behind me, taking it in turns to bump into me or push me. I was terrified of what they were planning for as soon as we were out of sight of St Mark's.

The further we got from school, the faster I walked. They kept right behind me, baying at my heels. The bus was already at the stop. I jumped on.

I was saved only because I saw an older kid I knew was already on the bus. I walked straight to him and sat next to him. He saw what was going on and told my tormentors to back off. It worked but it was a humiliating experience to have to be rescued like that, and when I was back in school the next day the bullying carried on. I was pushed over and tripped up with clockwork regularity. The teachers saw it happen from time to time but beyond telling the bullies off if they actually caught them in the act, they made no real effort to stop it. After Mum found out, she tried calling one of the bullies' mothers. That didn't work either. When Pete heard, his response was to tell me to 'just fucking hit them', but I couldn't do that. I felt paralysed when the bullies surrounded me and ashamed that I was so weak I couldn't stand up to them.

So the bullying escalated and, every day, I shrank a little further into myself. I couldn't see any way to make my life better without breaking my promise to Mum. I had to stay out of trouble.

All I could do was pray I made it to the end of term.

*

The Michael Maisey who came home from his last day in year seven was pathetic and broken. I took off my school uniform and threw it on the floor. The holidays stretched ahead – six weeks of freedom – but all I could think about was that day in September when the holidays would be over and the bullying would start over again.

Mum asked why I was looking so miserable. I couldn't tell her. I didn't want to worry her any more than I already had. I'd let her think that her phone call to one of my tormentors' mums had made a difference and everything was really OK.

By now we were living in a house of our own on the Richmond Road. A few houses along from where we lived was a family that we sort of knew. Jake, the son of the house, was older than me by a few years. When I was twelve, he was about fifteen. A huge gulf at that age but, while most kids in his year ignored the younger ones like me, Jake was always friendly. Though I didn't know it until years later, he'd also had a tough time as a child, with alcohol issues affecting his family. Perhaps that's why we connected. Deep down he recognized my vulnerability. We didn't have to say anything out loud.

We'd played together as much younger kids but I hadn't had much to do with Jake for a while when that summer came round. He seemed really grown up to me. All the same, when I walked past his house one afternoon he reached out to me, and invited me to join him and his mates.

I was flattered and pleased. I hopped over the wall to join him and the others – Clinton, Duwayne and Taylor – in the garden. They were just hanging out there. Drinking, smoking weed, play-fighting and chatting to any girls who would give them the time of day. They might have been intimidating –

Clinton was built like a rugby player, Duwayne had serious attitude – but they gave me a can of lager and as I drank it I started to relax. They seemed to like me.

Over the next few days, I opened up to Jake about the bullying I'd faced at school that term.

'I'll fucking bang them up, bruv!' was Jake's reaction.

I was shocked by the violence of his response. But Jake assured me that he'd got my back. I straight away felt so much confidence and relief just hearing him say that.

Jake promised me that he would show me how to make sure I didn't get bullied again. I don't know what motivated him to try to help me. Maybe he'd been through something similar himself. Whatever his reasons, he seemed determined to help me and heaven knows I needed help. In his back garden he had weights and a weights bench. Though I was still a skinny little kid, he soon got me lifting way more than I ever believed I could. He had a punch bag too. He showed me how to land my punches properly, causing maximum damage to the other guy without hurting myself in the process. We'd also 'slap box', which taught me how to move to keep out of harm's way. Every time I managed to land a punch on Jake – albeit playfully – my confidence grew. He enjoyed being my teacher.

Being with Jake and his mates that summer gave me something I'd been searching for most of my life. Up until then, my interactions with men had been largely negative. I'd been abused, shouted at, shaken, hit and bullied by adult men who should have been looking after me. I'd never felt completely safe. I'd never felt unconditionally supported by any man.

Jake and his mates offered me that support. Though it may have looked on the outside as though we spent that summer just mucking around, they were surprisingly nurturing. For the first time in as long as I could remember, I felt like I belonged. They listened to my worries about the bullying at school and offered solutions. Those solutions may not have been the 'right' ones, but they gave me hope that the next term could be different.

With Jake on my side, I made a conscious decision that something was going to change. *I* was going to change. Slowly, I began to build an entirely new character for myself from the best bits of each of my new friends. I wanted Jake's swagger with the ladies and his sharp wit. I wanted to be able to laugh off insults and banter like Taylor could. I wanted to be as laid-back as Duwayne, the carefree stoner. I wanted to be as intimidating as Clinton, who punctuated his calm demeanour with occasional explosive violence. His unpredictability gave him power. These were my new role models and I took them very seriously indeed.

At twelve, I was by far the youngest kid hanging out in Jake's front garden that summer. They were living a life that I aspired to. They listened to the Wu-Tang Clan, Biggie Smalls and Tupac Shakur. However, they weren't just pretending to be gangsters, like the kids in my year at school. Jake and his friends were starting to live the gangster life for real.

I soon found out that they were dealing drugs on behalf of much older guys. Men such as Reece, a huge black guy who had a reputation as a big-time criminal, or Tyrone, who would die in police custody years later when he swallowed his supply to keep it hidden and suffered a massive overdose as a result. The police were always around, driving past Jake's house or by the shops where we used to hang out together, trying to nail Reece or Tyrone. Never quite pulling it off.

Of course, I'd been drunk before and I'd tried cigarettes, but Jake and his mates introduced me to new ways to leave my worries behind. There were always drugs to be had and, though Reece and Tyrone tried to extract promises from Jake that I would not be allowed to have any of the drugs they sold, it wasn't long before I had my first spliff.

Jake rolled the thin white joint, making sure that it was tight and neat. He twisted one end and put the other end in his mouth. I watched as he lit the twist with his lighter and waited for the paper to burn down to the tobacco. He took a deep drag and smiled.

'That's so good,' he murmured. He took another drag and then passed the joint on to me.

I wasn't sure what to do.

'Just smoke it like it's a normal fag but try to hold the smoke in for longer,' Jake instructed.

I sucked in a mouthful of smoke and puffed out my cheeks as I tried to draw it down into my lungs and hold it there. Jake laughed at the look on my face.

'You can breathe out now,' he said.

How long until it would work? I wanted to know. And how would it work for me? I was used to getting drunk now. Would this feel any different?

It did.

It wasn't long before I started to feel the effects, and when I did I loved them. It was brilliant. I took to it straight away. It both calmed me down and cheered me up. I loved the feeling of getting out of my head, of floating above the shitty world I lived in. It was an even quicker way to check out than downing a few cans of cider. I couldn't stop giggling. My new friends loved to see me getting stoned. I was their mascot. Their pet. The joint went round the gang and came back to me again and again. I lay down on the grass and looked up at the sky, wondering why everyone didn't just get stoned every day. I wanted that feeling to stay with me for the rest of my life.

That spliff was just the beginning. Jake's gang had access to so much more than the odd bit of weed. I tried speed. I took ecstasy. I snorted coke and smoked it, sprinkled onto a joint. By the end of the summer there was very little I hadn't done. Despite the warnings of the dealers, I tried a little bit of everything.

Mum and Pete were too busy to notice what was going on with me. They had two small children to care for. Pete was always working to pay the bills. Mum was still drinking. When I went home, I would try to get past her as quickly as possible before she smelled anything on me or saw how I was weaving as I walked. She had her own worries and I was way down the list.

6

Jake and I were in the garden shed at my house. We were smoking weed and drinking, as usual. I had no fear around drugs anymore. I'd spent the summer in a happy haze. I didn't worry about the potential for side effects or an overdose. In fact, I wondered what all the fuss was about. I knew my limits when it came to getting stoned. I'd never passed out. I'd never even been sick. I thought I could handle anything. Whatever Jake suggested I try, I wanted. I was still only twelve years old but thanks to Jake's misguided mentorship – after all, he was just a kid himself – I was acting twice my age.

Maybe it was time to try the really hard stuff.

'You want to try crack?'

'Are you kidding?' I asked.

'No. I got some from Reece. Want to try it?'

'Sure.' I shrugged like it was no big deal.

Jake nodded. 'OK.'

He got the kit out. I'd heard him and the others talking about smoking crack before but I had never actually seen it. Unlike weed or speed or coke, crack was hard to get hold of. It was expensive too. It had a mystique about it. A dangerous mystique. As Jake prepared my first ever hit, I felt my heart pounding.

There were plenty of reasons to be scared of smoking crack cocaine. That day I was mostly scared that Mum or Pete would walk into the shed and catch us at it.

Jake had got this tiny rock from Tyrone the dealer, who handed it over as a kind of bonus for some favours Jake had done him. He had been adamant that none of it should end up in my hands.

'Make sure he doesn't have any,' Tyrone had told Jake specifically.

Tyrone was dating a girl who lived on my street. She was friends with Mum. They often drank together. For that reason alone, Tyrone didn't want me getting into trouble with drugs he'd supplied. But hearing that he didn't want me using crack only made me more determined. If Tyrone found out, he wouldn't say anything to Mum.

Jake held his lighter to the rock, making it flare at the edges. The smoke curled in the air as though it was a living creature. I took a deep breath and sucked it in.

I lay back and let it roll over me. In a summer of firsts, this was definitely the best. It was better than a first proper kiss. I was definitely in love. It was like nothing I could have imagined. Like ecstasy and weed rolled into one. It was a shame it was so quick. That first time the buzz lasted less than a minute, but it was like opening a window onto heaven.

There wasn't much to smoke that day. Just enough to spoil me regarding other softer drugs forever. I instantly wanted more.

'That's the problem,' Jake explained.

Though Jake was hardly careful about letting me try any kind of drugs he could get hold of, he made sure I knew that smoking crack is different to smoking a spliff or even a joint sprinkled with coke. You can't just smoke crack then get into bed to sleep it off, he told me. You've got to bring yourself down from a crack high carefully, otherwise you go crazy, doing whatever you can to keep the high going. You'll do anything to get a bit more.

That day there was no more, and Jake showed me how to balance the high with weed and alcohol – mostly cans of Stella Artois. I quickly understood Jake was right: you had to dilute the buzz so that you could walk away from the crack without going insane. I was already wondering when I'd get the chance to smoke it again. But I didn't have a job or even regular pocket money. I couldn't afford it.

Jake was leading me down the wrong path but I had never felt so good about myself as I did that summer and it was definitely because of his influence. I'd never felt like any man had my back before. Now I felt like part of a crazy family who would always stick up for me.

But at the same time as getting into drugs, I was getting into another crime. Shoplifting.

It was mostly food to begin with. Isleworth was just a short walk from places like Richmond, where people like Mick Jagger lived in huge houses backing onto the deer park. It was so close and yet it was like another world. It might as well have been on a different planet to the Ivybridge Estate.

As I got older, I resented the people who lived in Richmond. Everything they had seemed better and forever out of reach for someone like me. Even their food looked tastier than what we had to eat. I'd walk into the Marks and Spencer food hall and see all this stuff that Mum and Pete could never afford to buy.

I was fed up of having my nose pressed against the window. As my summer with Jake continued, I decided that I wasn't going to be that kid anymore. I wasn't going to be bullied at school and I wasn't going to take the condescension of the Richmond snobs anymore either. A sense of resentment had been building up inside me for a while. Those rich people had what I wanted and I was going to take it, starting with the food at M&S. I was going to even things up.

Jake showed me how it was done. The best thing was not to be seen. The second-best thing was to be able to run like Sebastian Coe if you were.

It usually went like this. We would walk into the shop as casually as we could, talking to each other and making jokes, careful to look natural. We'd pick stuff up like we were intending to pay for it and then, as we turned the corner of an aisle, which formed a kind of blind spot, we'd stuff the things we'd picked up into our pockets. With our pockets full, we'd make our way to the door, stopping to look at the stuff on the shelves closest to the exit. As soon as the coast was clear, we'd walk out as calmly as we could. Running would have drawn too much attention. A calm exit didn't raise suspicions. I had an angelic face too, which helped.

I stole stuff to eat but I stole socks and boxers as well. And I soon moved on to stealing alcohol. When it came to stealing from off-licences, I didn't do things subtly. How could I? I was twelve years old and I looked it. I wasn't even supposed to be in an offy and I definitely couldn't pretend otherwise. I relied mostly on grabbing the six-pack nearest to the door and being able to outrun whoever was behind the counter.

Shoplifting gave me stuff to barter with. I could swap cans

for cigarettes – I was smoking around fifteen a day – or weed or cash. There was a proper black market going on among the kids in the borough. Having cash in my hand made me feel especially good. It gave me independence and power. I felt like a proper gangster. And as much as I loved the cash, I loved the adrenalin rush I got from taking what others had. It was like a big 'fuck you' to the system which had let me down and the people who didn't know what it was like growing up in my world.

That summer I created a whole new personality. I was bigger, thanks to a growth spurt and lifting weights in Jake's garden. I was more skilled in fighting. I was more skilled in the art of not fighting too. Watching the older guys had taught me that a lot of battles were won by simply looking like you were ready to smack someone up. I thought nothing of taunting adult men who walked past Jake's house. Yet I was still worried about going back to school in September. Over the six-week-long holiday I'd built up that first day back in my mind to such a degree that, by the time it came round, I knew I wouldn't be able to get through it without some help.

The night before term started, I went to the off-licence and stole a bottle of Thunderbird, a fortified wine. The label was blue with silver writing. It tasted like nail polish remover but, at 21 per cent proof, I knew it would do the job. The following morning, while my sister Maria got ready for a new school term like she couldn't wait to be back there, I necked half the bottle of Thunderbird while I was getting dressed. It wasn't the ideal kind of breakfast. I put the bottle in my school bag and drank the rest on the way to the bus stop.

I could hold my drink by now so I wasn't drunk when I got

onto the bus, but I was definitely pumped with adrenalin. I made eye contact with Jackson – who was probably the weakest of the group who'd made my life hell – and deliberately banged into him as I walked past. He looked away. I could tell he was confused. That was enough to let me know that I had success-fully turned the tables. But I didn't stop there.

I'd worked myself up so much over the holidays that I was full of pent-up aggression. I had to express it. I was still worried that the scared child I had been would come back. I was convinced that my bullies must still be planning something more. That lunchtime I joined a football game on the team opposite Jackson and his friends. I took Jackson down with a rough tackle. I got up and walked away. He remained on the floor, looking up at me like he couldn't believe what had happened. We were like animals. I had shown domination, just as Jake had coached me. Jackson brushed himself off and walked away, cussing, but he didn't try to set the matter straight. He could tell it might not go his way. It was enough.

A few weeks later, when parents' evening came around, Mrs Pirelli asked my mother what had happened to me over the holidays. I was sitting next to Mum at the time and I swelled with pride at the thought that my transformation had been noticed.

'It's like he's a completely different child,' Mrs Pirelli complained.

I'm here to stay, bitch, said the voice inside my head.

I slouched in my chair, smirking at Mrs Pirelli's confusion.

Mum was embarrassed. She tried to defend herself, telling Mrs Pirelli that she would sort it out. I'd been having a few problems with kids on the estate, that was all. On the way home, she was angry and tried to tell me that I'd seen the last of Jake, but I wasn't going to take any notice of that. Even if she hit me with the wooden spoon that was used for smacking more often than cooking. Even if Pete tried to back her up by screaming in my face. I just didn't care anymore. The old Michael was gone and the new Michael's motto was 'fuck the world'.

7

Far from staying away from Jake as Mum tried to insist, that term I spent more time in his company than ever. Whenever I was out of school I was round there. Sometimes, I walked out of school during the day and went straight to Jake's house.

On this particular day, though, we were in the garden shed at Mum and Pete's again. We'd already smoked some crack. This time, for the comedown, Jake suggested something different. We weren't going to have a drink and a spliff like we usually did. This time, we were going to smoke heroin.

Jake added the heroin to a joint. He took a drag himself then passed it to me.

I sucked it down into my lungs. I didn't feel anything at first. I was ready to tell Jake it was all a waste of time. But over the next fifteen minutes the sensation I'd been waiting for started to creep over me.

I lay back against a pile of old rubbish, oblivious to my surroundings. I said to myself, *If I'm dying now, I really don't fucking care.* I felt warm and relaxed. I was enveloped in what I can only describe as a feeling of complete love. Nothing I had ever experienced came near it. More than twenty years later, hardly anything I've experienced since comes near that first hit of heroin.

It was an out-of-body experience. A rush of love and well-being so pure that I wanted to stay in that space forever. It was as if I had gone to heaven. A place where there was no trauma. A place where I couldn't be hurt. A place where all the bad stuff that dogged me when my mind was clear simply disappeared. It was like falling asleep without losing consciousness. Everything was perfect.

My muscles melted. Warmth flooded my limbs. Forget alcohol, forget weed, forget crack. This was how I wanted to feel forever.

Jake was laughing at me but I didn't care. The sound of his laughter seemed so far away, like an echo. I didn't care how I looked to him. I didn't care about anything. I'd found the love of my life.

When I came back down, I was excited.

'Wow,' was pretty much all I managed to say.

Before I took heroin, I'd not been able to comprehend that such a good feeling existed. That I even had it inside me to feel that way. I knew at once that I would have to do it again.

'When can I do more?'

As it happened, I didn't take heroin again for a long time after that. Not until I began dealing myself in my late teens. I was lucky that Jake didn't have any more to share with me while I was so young. It takes just a few days to become dependent on heroin. It takes a lifetime to shake that dependency off.

I was continuing to shoplift and most of the time I was getting away with it. Then, of course, I got caught big time. It was in Marks and Spencer Richmond again. I was with a kid who lived down the road from me. He wasn't as experienced as I was and he was probably the reason we were rumbled. He didn't know how to look casual. The security guard, an old Irish man, grabbed me by the collar and dragged me to his office where we waited for the police. Though I'd seen the police plenty of times while hanging out with Jake and his mates, this was the first time they'd come for me.

I was handcuffed and walked to the station. Though it was only about fifty metres away from the shop, it felt like miles. All the posh people of Richmond looked on in horror as I was paraded by them. A common criminal.

The police officer probably thought that my very public walk of shame would be enough to embarrass me back onto the straight and narrow, but looking back, I can see how it only fuelled my sense of alienation.

I was given a caution. My first. There was no conversation as to why I was shoplifting. No friendly face to try to tease out what was going wrong. Because I was under sixteen, Mum had to come to the station to be with me. She was not best pleased. Meanwhile Pete was raging. When we got home he told me that I needed to shape up or leave. He didn't want me around the younger kids. His devotion to them was absolute. If I was a danger to his son and daughter, then I would have to go. He'd kick me out no problem. Didn't matter to him where I went, he said. He'd be happy to see me go into care. It was all so much hot air to me. I thought he was bullshitting.

Seeing how little Pete's threats seemed to affect me, Mum decided that I needed to be forced to face the reality of my behaviour so she arranged for a police officer to call at the house to give me a talking-to.

*

It was a Saturday afternoon. Everyone else was out. Pete must have taken Maria, Sophie and Justin somewhere else. Though I've got no doubt Justin would have loved to meet a real-life policeman, it's understandable that Pete didn't want them to meet one under these circumstances and have to answer difficult questions afterwards. So, it was just me and Mum.

The officer arrived. Though I was getting to know the local police better than Mum would have wanted – since that first caution, I'd been the subject of frequent 'random' stop and searches – I didn't know this officer. He was in his forties and had come over from Twickenham. Mum invited him in and offered him tea and biscuits. She'd made an effort not to drink that day, so that it looked like I came from a normal, wholesome sort of home.

We sat in the living room and he gave me the talk. It was basically a lecture. He spoke and I listened. Or at least, I was supposed to listen. I was already too far gone to be scared by the kind of things he was telling me. It was the same old speech. I'd already heard it from Mum and Pete a thousand times.

'You're on course to ruin your life,' the police officer said. 'You keep on carrying on the way you are, you're going to end up in Feltham Young Offenders.'

I knew about Feltham Young Offenders, of course. The first time I heard about it, I was really young. I was about seven or eight years old. The way it came about is pretty sad. Maria and I had been playing with some other kids on the estate and I'd kissed one of the girls. She was a couple of years younger than me, maybe six. It was just a quick kiss. Part of a game. But when Maria told Mum about it, Mum went ballistic. She told me that if I did anything like that again I would be going to prison. Then she loaded me into the back of the car and drove me to Feltham.

As young as I was, I found the whole experience pretty frightening. I'd never seen a building as big or forbidding as that prison. It was vast. I stared at the fences that surrounded it and was both scared and fascinated.

'That's where you'll go,' Mum said.

To me, kissing the girl down the street was just a game. To Mum, it was a sign of something worse. You see, it wasn't just the adults who abused the kids in the Nazareth home where Mum had grown up. The older kids abused the younger kids too. There was no innocence in a game of kiss chase to Mum. It seems like an overreaction but to Mum the danger was real. If only she'd applied the same logic to Uncle Tommy.

Now here I was being threatened with Feltham again. Mum seemed pleased with the way the 'conversation' with the police officer had gone, though I hardly said a word. She hoped that what he'd said would be enough to convince me to drop Jake and concentrate on my studies again.

It didn't work. I felt lectured, talked down to and the angry part of me that hated to be patronized only got angrier. Perhaps if the police officer had asked Mum to leave the room that afternoon, and talked to me and only me, it would have been different. As it was, he said only what she wanted to hear and not what I *needed* to hear. And he didn't pick up what was really going on at all. Mum had convinced him that I was a good boy from a good family who just needed a little scare.

The police officer told me how lucky I was to have a mum who cared so much. I smiled at that but said nothing. Inside my head, a voice hissed, *This motherfucker has no fucking idea.*

The woman who stood before him pretending to be such a good mother was the same woman who could often be found sitting on a bench by the river drinking Diamond White with the local homeless drunks. She thought she kept it a secret but we'd all seen her stumbling up the road afterwards. She was such a hypocrite.

Just get the fuck out, mate, my inner voice told the policeman. *I'm going to do what the fuck I want to do and you ain't gonna stop me.*

I was beginning to get a reputation in the neighbourhood. After the caution I only went up in the eyes of the kids around Isleworth. It wasn't the police officer's lecture that convinced me, but I was spending less time with Jake. We were all getting older and he wanted to go to places I couldn't get into – clubs and pubs, etc. But there was another gang of kids coming up in the neighbourhood, younger guys who looked at me and thought I was some kind of hero. With Jake I'd had an apprenticeship in becoming a real mean motherfucker. I'd taken on the bullies and gone from scared little boy to all-out angry thug. Now I had some students of my own.

When the police officer left that afternoon, I grabbed my coat and a can of Mum's Diamond White and headed straight out to the benches near the local shops where my new gang of crazies hung out. I made them laugh as I described the officer's attempts to persuade me to change my ways. I widened my eyes as I described the horrors of Feltham.

'Like I'm scared of that.'

I was in my element.

8

I needed to up the stakes.

The idea first came to me while I was at Jake's house. His mum was out. We were inside, smoking and getting high. I was still only fifteen years old. Someone had brought round a DVD of *Menace II Society*, an American teen crime drama set in the Los Angeles projects. Though Isleworth was a long way from LA, I identified strongly with the kids in the film, who were trapped into a life of gang violence and crime.

I loved the music. I loved the way they dressed. The way they talked. There was a glamour to the danger they lived with. They got girls, money, respect. Their struggles seemed heroic to me. They seemed real.

There was a scene in the film in which one of the characters – a black kid with dreadlocks – walked into a shop to buy some stuff. He chose what he wanted, paid for it, then, as he was leaving, he heard the shopkeeper insult him. In reaction, he simply turned around, took out a gun and shot the shopkeeper in the face. Just like that. Instant revenge.

It got me thinking. I was still shoplifting. Still running out of off-licences with all the cans and bottles I could carry. If I had a gun, I could walk into a shop and take whatever I wanted. Not just booze and cigarettes but cash out of the till. I was tired of trying to turn the stuff I shoplifted into money. It was small-scale stuff and I was getting bored of it. I decided that I had to have a gun.

But I didn't live in LA. It wasn't so easy to get hold of a gun in 1990s London. When I told Jake, he laughed. He couldn't help me get hold of one. It was the realm of serious gangsters, not kids like us. Not even adult drug dealers like Reece or Tyrone could obtain a firearm easily. But I wasn't to be put off. I would improvise.

In the Treaty Centre shopping mall in Hounslow, there was a branch of Clinton Cards. In the window was a display of lighters, which included one shaped like a handgun. It was just a replica. When you pulled the trigger, instead of a bullet, a flame came out of the end of the barrel, ready for your cigarette. But it looked so real. If you didn't know it was a lighter, you wouldn't take your chances with anyone who waved it in your face. That was what I thought.

I went into the card shop and looked at that replica gun day after day. I couldn't afford to buy it. I would have shoplifted it, but because it was pretty much the most expensive thing in the whole shop it was kept in a locked display cabinet. Still, I asked the assistant to get it out of the cabinet for me so I could take a closer look. I told her I was thinking of getting it for my dad. I held it reverently and turned it this way and that, looking for a reason why I didn't really want it. It was no good, I loved that lighter. It was perfect. A flawless copy of a real gun.

And pretty soon it belonged to me. My girlfriend at the time saw how interested I was in it and so she saved up to buy it as a Christmas gift. She didn't have a clue why I really wanted it. To her, it was just a nice present. Something she knew I'd be pleased to receive. To me, it was the key to a whole new world of crime.

I loved that fake gun. I carried it on my hip and, even though I knew it wasn't real, I felt powerful when I had it on me. I even took it in to school, walking around like the kids in *Menace II Society*. It gave me a swagger. I already had a reputation for being crazy thanks to the way I had dealt with the kids who used to pick on me. Then there was the shoplifting and the various street fights I got into. As the rumour went round school that I had a firearm, no one was willing to get on my bad side anymore.

I watched *Menace II Society* obsessively. I also watched *Goodfellas*. Once again, I was trying to build a new character for myself, modelling my actions on what I saw on the screen.

There's a scene in *Goodfellas* where the hero's girlfriend gets groped by a sleazebag. The hero reacts by smashing the groper in the face with the butt of his gun. I studied the way he did it. The way he jabbed the butt into his victim's nose, spreading a bloody mess across his face. I practised my moves in the mirror. There was so much power in having a gun even if you didn't fire it. Even if you *couldn't* fire it.

In those days, I walked around Isleworth as though I was starring in my own gangster movie. A few weeks later, I was down by the shops with the gang of kids my age who'd decided at some point to make me their leader. We were all around fifteen years old now. We were drinking and smoking, getting drunk and high. One of our little gang, a kid called Ricky

Shields, was being particularly mouthy, shouting obscenities at random passers-by. Most of them ignored him but then he got into it with a bloke who was in the phone box trying to make a call. The bloke was drunk. When he came out of the phone box, he tried to have a go at Ricky for bothering him. He started pushing him in the chest.

'What do you think you're playing at, you little shit?' he said.

Seeing how much bigger than him the bloke was now that they were toe to toe, Ricky held his hands up in submission.

'Sorry, mate,' he said. 'I didn't mean any harm.'

Ricky's apology was not accepted. The bloke carried on jabbing at Ricky and pushing him backwards. Though Ricky was still on his feet, I could tell he was getting scared. The bloke was big and he was angry. He had turned on Ricky like a bear turning on a fly.

When Ricky stumbled as the bloke pushed him again, I saw red. No matter that Ricky had provoked him. The way that bloke was picking on my mate, who was so much smaller than he was, reminded me of all the times I'd been on the receiving end of a grown man's aggression. It reminded me of Tommy, of Sid, of Pete. Of Dad. The bloke grabbed Ricky by the neck of his sweater and pulled back his fist, ready to pummel him. I jumped up.

The drunk bloke towered over me too, but I didn't care. Right then he represented everything I hated. It was time for me to push back. I had my secret weapon tucked into my belt. I shoved Ricky out of the way and went for the bloke.

Using the gun, I smacked the bloke hard in the face. I got lucky and his nose bust apart instantly. He staggered backwards, with his hands covering his broken nose, blood pouring down the front of his shirt. The shock put him straight out of action. He crumpled to the floor. I felt incredible – fearless, strong, high on adrenalin. I would have hit him again but my friends pulled me off and together we legged it away from the scene of the crime. Whatever the provocation, they knew I had gone too far. There was too much blood.

Later, when we went back to the square, we found the area where I'd attacked the drunk bloke fenced off with fluttering police tape. There was still blood on the floor. A policeman was still asking passers-by if they had any information. He didn't seem to notice us.

It gave me a kick to see that the police had been called. I wasn't especially worried about it. My mates weren't going to grass on me. There were no witnesses. All the same, it seemed like a good idea to lie low for a while.

I avoided the square for a bit, hanging out instead at a nearby park, where a rope swing attracted big gangs of kids from all over the borough. One of them was Chelsea.

I really liked her, though she went to a posh school and might have been considered way out of my league. Amazing as it seemed to me at the time, she liked me too. We arranged that I would meet her after school one day and take her to McDonald's.

I wasn't the only boy who thought Chelsea was stunning. Chelsea was widely considered to be the hottest girl in her school so it was no surprise to find I had competition in the shape of Ice Man, the toughest guy. I forget his real name but Ice Man suited him. His head was square like an ice cube. Anyway, somehow he got to hear that Chelsea was interested in me, and when I turned up to meet her for our Maccy D's date Ice Man cornered me outside the school gates and challenged me to a fight. Just like that. Still high on breaking the nose of the bloke in the phone box, I felt invincible. I readily accepted Ice Man's challenge.

It was a bad move for both of us. As the hardest kid in his school, Ice Man had plenty of friends ready to back him up, but I had an equal number of kids ready to stand behind me. When we next met by the school gates a few days later we had both come mob-handed. This wasn't just a one-on-one fight. It had the potential to turn into a war.

Our friends formed a circle around us. Chelsea stood with a small group of girls, her best mates, chewing anxiously on a fingernail. I was sure that she wanted me to win and I was certain that I could. I was going to be her champion, like a knight in a jousting competition or a gladiator in the Colosseum.

The two sides of the crowd shouted and jeered at one another as Ice Man and I squared up in the middle. I'd drunk a couple of cans to get myself ready. As the adrenalin began to rise, I clenched my jaw and snarled at my enemy. He laughed at me. I told myself he wouldn't be laughing long. I had to believe that. He was bigger than I remembered.

It seemed like we stood there staring at each other for an age. Ice Man threw the first punch. I tried to duck it but he caught me a glancing blow on the cheek. When I came back from that, I swung for him and soon we were smacking each other like it was a matter of life or death.

Ice Man had earned his reputation as a hard man but he had no idea what he was dealing with. He might have been king of his school but I'd honed my skills on the street. I was punching with the weight of years of anger behind me. Like the man in the phone box, Ice Man wasn't just a kid I'd fallen out with. He was all the people who'd let me down. It was like I was acting. Right then I was the hero of the film in my head. Ice Man was the bad guy who thought he could bully me. I was the good guy pushed too far.

I got a hit straight to his face. For a second, Ice Man stared at me and it was like it was all happening in slow motion. It was as though a red mist descended. All the anger inside me was concentrated into my fists. Then Ice Man went down like he'd been shot and, while he was down, I continued to hit him, smacking him with everything I had, until he rolled into a foetal position and covered his head with his arms, and friends on both sides rushed in to pull me off him. Chelsea and Ice Man's teachers had got wind of what was happening and were on their way to break things up. If they hadn't, I don't know what would have happened.

Chelsea was horrified. When I stood up and looked at her, she covered her eyes with her hands and turned away. Her girl-friends closed around her and ushered her back behind the safety of the school gates. While I just stood there gazing after her, my own friends shook me back to my senses and suggested that we leg it as a matter of urgency. Someone had called the police.

By now, my reputation was spreading beyond Isleworth to Twickenham and Richmond. People were saying that I was in a different league. I wasn't just tough or dangerous. I was properly mad.

I was arrested for the attack on Ice Man, of course. It was bound to happen. There were loads of witnesses and a lot of them were Ice Man's mates. When I was taken into the station, I admitted to having had a fight – I couldn't have done otherwise; too many people had seen it happen – but I said I only hit Ice Man in self-defence.

'He started it.'

The police seemed to want to believe it. They decided the whole thing was just a fight between two schoolkids, nothing worth getting worked up about. The charge was dropped and I was allowed to go home with a strict warning to stay away from Chelsea's school. I felt invincible.

However, I was beginning to understand that having a reputation like mine wasn't without cost. Now people I liked were starting to avoid me. Chelsea refused even to speak to me again. Far from seeing me as a knight in shining armour, fighting to win her hand, she simply saw me as a thug who'd smashed her friend's face in.

Still, I didn't dial it back. Instead, I moved to the next level.

9

I decided it was time to use the gun for the reasons I'd first wanted to get it. I'd lost all perspective on reality. The only thing I cared about was becoming the toughest and most respected kid in the borough. I was obsessed with the kind of power I thought the kids in *Menace II Society* had. I was in a full-blown 'fuck the world' state of mind.

With the gun in my hand, I didn't need money. I could walk into anywhere and take what I wanted. I decided it was time to do a proper robbery. I was going to walk into a shop and get them to empty the till.

I knew it wouldn't be quite that simple, though. I had to choose my target carefully. For a start, I had to find a shop that wasn't too close to home to minimize the risk of being seen by someone who knew me. So I chose a couple of places a fair distance away from where I lived and went into them a few times to check out the staff. How many were there? Who was behind the till? A man? A woman? Young or old? Did they look like they might be crazy enough to put up any kind of resistance to someone who'd just pulled a gun on them?

After a week or so of surveillance, I chose my first target – a corner shop in another borough – and started to psych myself up. On the day itself I hung out on a street nearby for an hour, watching who was coming and going. I knew there was usually just one man on the till. Middle-aged and out of shape. I could easily outrun him.

As I waited for the exact right time to strike, I drank three cans of Stella and smoked a joint to steady my nerves. But just as I was about to pull on my balaclava and go in, a delivery van turned up. By the time the delivery guy had finished in the shop and driven off, the moment was gone. I'd already spent too long hanging around. With every extra minute the risk of being clocked looking suspicious had grown so I gave up and I went home.

Yes, I planned my first robbery to the nth degree. I did my research meticulously. I had my rules. I'd never try to rob a shop with more than one sales assistant. I'd never go in while a customer was inside. I'd always choose targets outside my own borough. Too many people knew me in Isleworth. Too many people wanted to take me down, including some of the police. I knew I couldn't afford to give them an excuse to do so.

Until the day I did.

That night one of my friends was having a party. Everyone I knew would be there, plus a girl I had my eye on. I wanted to get my hair cut so I'd go to my mate's bash looking my best. When I'd told her about it, Mum had promised to give me the money to go to the hairdresser's, but when it came to the morning of the party she refused.

'Why?'

I could tell she'd been drinking. She must have spent all the cash I was hoping she'd give me on booze. Ironically, Mum was working as a care assistant at a place called Nazareth House in those days. She'd been out with one of her colleagues, Lynn, the night before. She was still pissed in the morning.

Anyway, we had a stupid argument about it. Mum turned it from being about her drinking into a row about my behaviour. She didn't remember having made any promises.

'Come on, Mum,' I said. 'You can't remember because you're pissed.'

That was a red rag to a bull.

'How dare you! I am not drunk.'

'You're always fucking drunk. Then you make promises you can't follow up, like you're doing now.'

I had zero respect for my mother. She'd let me down too often. It was clear she cared more for my half-siblings than me and Maria. I think that's why it hurt more when she didn't keep her drunken promises. Every time she told me she'd do something for me, I thought the balance was going to be evened up. I thought she was going to prove she cared. I was only asking for a couple of quid but in my mind it represented so much more.

'I didn't promise you any bloody money,' she carried on. 'Why would I? You're not getting anything until I start seeing you pull your weight around the house.'

That was the end of it as far as Mum was concerned.

It was still early in the morning. I left Mum to sleep off her hangover and went upstairs to get my trusty balaclava. And my gun.

I was angry and because I was angry I made a stupid mistake. Fuck waiting for Mum to cough up. I didn't need her. I decided that I would get the money I wanted by robbing a corner shop within walking distance of home.

The shop wasn't such an unreasonable target. It was a news-agent's tucked away from the main road. It was quiet. It was a Saturday morning. Isleworth was still waking up. I knew that it was unlikely there would be more than one person on the till at that time in the morning.

The street was empty. I was still angry. I didn't really think about my getaway strategy. I wanted to get the money and to get on with my day. I walked up to the shop, pulling on my balaclava as I pushed open the door. There was an Asian woman behind the counter. As I predicted, she was on her own.

When I saw her, I faltered for a moment. She was small and old and looked frail and I was about to pull a gun on her. For a split second I considered turning round and walking out without saying anything, but I was already right there with my balaclava on. She was already screaming. The damage was half done by then. I might as well get the cash.

'Open the till,' I barked at her, as I held the gun steady at head height.

'No,' she refused. I was shocked. She may have looked weak but she was almost as crazy as I was. 'Go away!' she screamed at me.

'Open the till,' I tried again.

'No I won't! Go away! Help! Help! Thief!'

She was yelling the place down. It was just a matter of time before someone heard her. There was a flat above the shop. There might be someone up there who would be down any minute.

'Open the till,' I tried one more time. 'Or I'll fucking shoot you.'

Grandma pulled herself up to her full height.

'No,' she told me.

Then: scream, scream, scream.

There was nothing I could do. I wasn't going to hit her. I definitely couldn't shoot her. I had no choice but to grab what I could from the counter and get out of there. I snatched a couple of cigarette packets. It was a disaster.

And it was going to get worse.

I pulled off my balaclava as I ran from the shop. There's nothing like someone wearing a balaclava when there isn't a snowstorm to draw attention. But I hadn't properly checked that the coast was clear before I stepped out onto the street. As it was, I walked straight into one of the shop's paperboys, returning with his empty bag. He skidded his bike to a halt right in front of me. Even worse, I knew him. And he knew me.

His name was Arthur. He was older than me by about two years and went to a different school, but by then everyone around my age in Isleworth knew exactly who I was. The woman in the shop was still screaming. Now I had to make sure Arthur kept his mouth shut. I showed him the gun.

'You fucking say anything and I will kill you,' I hissed.

Arthur looked at the ground, making sure not to meet my eye.

'I'll fucking kill you.'

I got out of there as fast as I could.

What a fuck-up.

I went home. Ironically Mum was in a better mood and she gave me the money for a haircut after all. I got it done and went to the party as planned. I tried not to dwell on what had happened that morning. I told myself that it didn't matter that Arthur had seen me. The woman in the shop had only seen a man in a balaclava. She couldn't identify me. Arthur wouldn't dare. He knew it wasn't worth it. If he did grass me up and I wasn't able to get to him myself, I had plenty of friends who would.

So, I went to the party and I had a good weekend, all things considered. I put the robbery gone wrong behind me. Nothing would come of it except that I'd had a big reminder that I shouldn't risk shitting on my own doorstep.

I partied all through the weekend and for much of the following week. I bunked off school and hung out with my mates until late. By the time Thursday night rolled around, I'd pretty much forgotten that the botched robbery happened at all. I went to bed that night thinking about what I would be doing that weekend. I had no idea how the next few days were really going to pan out.

10

I was still asleep when they arrived. The flying squad. Mum answered the door. When she told them that I wasn't even awake, they told her to stay downstairs and keep quiet while they delivered a very personal wake-up call.

While I slept on, completely unaware, three armed police officers let themselves into my bedroom and arranged themselves around my bed. I woke to find the barrel of a gun – a very real one this time – levelled at my nose.

'Sit up slowly,' said the officer in charge. 'Keep your hands where I can see them. Don't try anything funny.'

My heart was pounding as I slowly followed his directions, still not entirely sure I wasn't dreaming.

'Where is the firearm?' the officer asked me.

I knew there was no point mucking around. I told him where to find it. Two officers kept their weapons trained on me while the first officer retrieved the lighter. I could tell that he knew it was a fake as soon as he saw it, but that didn't mean he or the others would relax their approach.

'Get out of the bed.'

I stood in the middle of my bedroom wearing nothing but my underpants while three huge men in bulletproof vests discussed their next move. This was not how I'd expected my weekend to begin.

I was terrified. Honestly, I was scared for my life. Ironically, I'd never been at the wrong end of a gun before. I prayed the officers would drop the bad-cop act now they could see I was just a kid but they didn't. I didn't even get to put my own clothes on. The police bagged my gun as evidence and did the same with some of my clothes – my Schott jacket, my balaclava, my best trainers – while I was told to put on a white jumpsuit that made me look like I was contaminated. Then they escorted me downstairs.

Now for the worst bit. Facing my mum. I'd heard her shouting, waking the whole house. Maria was standing on the landing, eyes wide. Pete kept Sophie and Justin out of the way. I could only imagine what he would say when he got hold of me again. At the bottom of the stairs, in our narrow hallway, Mum tried to argue with the officers. They were treating me too roughly, she said. Couldn't they see I was just a child? The officers took no notice of her. They treated me like any grown man. A grown man suspected of a robbery.

'Be careful with him,' Mum pleaded as I was shuffled out through the front door.

Though it was still early, by now the entire street had turned out to see what was going on. Their gawping faces were full of secret delight. This was proper entertainment. I knew plenty of them thought I had it coming. I kept my head down as I was led to the van with my hands cuffed together.

I was taken to the police station in Chiswick. In the back of the van, with its covered windows, I was finally wide awake and the seriousness of the situation was beginning to sink in.

I'd been taken to the station before – for shoplifting, for that fight with Ice Man – but on those previous occasions the arresting officers had treated me like the kid I was. This felt different. There was no banter. No sense that I could cheek my way out of it like I had done in the past.

I was checked in at the reception desk and put into the first cell on the left because I was a juvenile and would need to be kept an eye on. The room was bare but for a bed and a metal toilet. I'd never been in a cell before and I already knew I didn't like it. However, I assumed I wouldn't be in there for long.

When the facts of the robbery came out, they'd let me off, I was sure. I hadn't used a real gun. I hadn't got away with anything significant. The woman behind the till was never in any real danger from me. I wouldn't have hurt her. But no one wanted to listen to my excuses this time.

A duty solicitor was summoned to explain what was happening and sit with me in my interview. She was a woman, Asian, relatively young. Probably not out of her twenties. She seemed disinterested in what I had to say in mitigation. She warned me that, because it was Friday, it would likely be Monday before I could be seen by a magistrate.

'What does that mean?' I asked.

'It means you'll have to spend the weekend in a cell.'

'No way!' I exclaimed. 'They can't keep me in there.'

The solicitor cast her eye over the charges again.

'I'm afraid they can. You're not here for shoplifting, Michael.'

For a second Arthur's frightened face flashed into my mind and I felt bad. But then I felt angry. When I did get out of that cell, Arthur was going to be the first to know about it.

The solicitor tucked her papers into her briefcase and wished the interviewing officers a good weekend.

I was taken back to the cell. I hadn't had any breakfast so the custody officer asked the kitchen to send something up. I sat on the bed with the tray on my lap. The food was all right. A cooked breakfast. Compared to the food I got at home, it didn't take much to be an improvement. Mum was no cook; her speciality was oven chips still frozen in the middle because she was too drunk to remember how long they'd been in. So I ate the breakfast hungrily, then lay down and wondered what would happen next.

The solicitor was joking, surely. They couldn't keep me in all weekend. I was certain that Mum would be doing her best to make sure that didn't happen. We knew enough people who'd been in trouble with the police. One of them would be able to tell her what to do, who to talk to. There was no way I'd be in the cell overnight.

Mum came to see me later that morning. Her eyes were red.

'How could you do this to us?' she hissed at me.

'How's Pete?' I asked.

'He's ready to kill you.'

'Am I going to be allowed home?'

'The solicitor says no. You've got to wait for the magistrate.'

I thought of the things I'd had planned. There was another party. My mates would be going. Maybe Arthur would be there. What I needed was to get a message out to him that if he insisted on identifying me, there were going to be consequences.

'So I'm really going to be here all fucking weekend?'

'Perhaps it'll do you some good,' Mum said.

*

That first night in custody, I didn't get much sleep. Even if I hadn't been worried about the situation, the bed wasn't what you could call comfortable. It was made to be easily cleaned. The plastic mattress was sticky and noisy whenever I tried to roll over. The blankets were plastic too and gave little warmth. It was impossible to wrap them round yourself properly. Add to that the fact that it was never properly dark in that cell, just as it never seemed properly light during the day. The tiny window on the outside world was opaque, like thick ice.

So I lay awake, staring at the ceiling where someone had stuck a sticker with the Crimestoppers number. For real or as a joke? I didn't know. By three in the morning I knew that number off by heart. I also knew I would never use it. Unlike Arthur, I was not a grass. I hoped he was having a sleepless night too, wondering what I would do to him when I got out of there. In the semi-darkness, I plotted my revenge. Arthur was a dead man walking as far as I was concerned.

Then it was morning again. The window in the cell door slid open.

'Wakey-wakey,' said the waggish guard.

I had less appetite for a cooked breakfast now.

'When do we get to go out for some exercise?' I asked.

The guard just laughed.

It was worse than I had ever imagined. There was nothing to do but wait. I had nothing to read. No one to talk to. I could only go over and over what had happened and worry how it would pan out if and when the police let me go. Pete would be going mental. Mum would have to kick me out. How would I survive if they really did chuck me out on the street? My tough-guy image was taking a real knock. When Mum came in to visit again, the first thing I did was promise her that if I got out, I was going to change.

'You better had,' she said.

On the Sunday evening, when the station had fallen quiet again after the rush of weekend drunk and disorderlies, I had another visitor. The local chief superintendent came in for a chat.

He sat down beside me and looked at me with an expression that was a mixture of pity and concern. It was the first time since my arrest that anyone except Mum had seemed worried for me.

'We've never had someone so young come in here for such a serious crime,' he told me.

I couldn't help feeling a little proud at that. Even the chief super thought I was a badass. He caught me smirking.

'It's not a joke. You're on a bad track, Michael.'

He echoed the speech of that officer who'd come to talk to me at home. I was throwing my life away. A criminal record would make it hard, if not impossible, for me to get a job, have a career, have a life.

'You're young now,' he said. 'You probably think this exciting. But in thirty years' time, you'll still be reaping the consequences. You'll look back and wish you'd done things differently.'

I nodded and made the right sounds. The chief superintendent patted me on the shoulder and left me alone again.

His pep talk went in one ear and out the other. I lay down on the bed again, rolled onto my side and stared at the wall for a change of view. I rehearsed the story I would tell the magistrate in my head. I would explain how it had all been a misunderstanding. I'd only been wearing a balaclava because I was cold. I didn't think how intimidating it would look to the woman behind the counter. She started screaming and didn't give me a chance to explain. I was going to pay for the cigarettes but forgot in the confusion. I waved the gun at Arthur as a joke. It wasn't a real gun. I was just messing around.

I was going to get off and, after that, I was going to be more careful. But I was not going to go back to school, get my GCSEs and become a fully functioning member of a system that was already loaded against me.

I was fifteen. I was in police custody. But I wasn't no mug.

11

On Monday morning, I was collected from Chiswick police station and taken to Brentford Magistrates' Court. Another van. More handcuffs. At least this time I was wearing my own clothes.

At the court, a few people had gathered to see me checked in. I think they wanted to know what an armed robber, just fifteen years old, would be like. There were two women and one man on duty that day. I could tell they were surprised by me. They'd been expecting a hard man. I still looked very much like a kid.

I was put in one of the court cells. It was a similar size to the cell I'd been in all weekend – the Victorians understood that even criminals need their space – but this one was underground with no natural light whatsoever. It was cold. I hoped it wouldn't be long before I was taken upstairs.

My mood was rapidly changing for the worse. Over the weekend I'd psyched myself up. I'd convinced myself that the strange luck I'd had so far when it came to my criminal activities would hold. In the van to the court, that gung-ho feeling had evaporated to be replaced by anxiety. What evidence that I didn't know about had the police gathered over the weekend? Was I in bigger trouble than I thought? What did that mean?

One of the court attendants, a woman, a grandmotherly type, took it upon herself to look after me. She looked in on me more often than she had to. Her smile was warm and genuine. Each time she asked if I wanted tea and a biscuit. It was a struggle not to tear up at her kindness.

My solicitor was not so kind or patient. She advised me to plead guilty.

'Don't waste time pretending you didn't do it. The evidence is overwhelming.'

It wasn't just that Arthur had identified me. There was CCTV from the shop. It was of the back of my head but I was still absolutely recognizable. I hadn't even noticed the camera. What an idiot I'd been.

That day, I was taken up to the court a couple of times as my case was processed. Mum was there in the public gallery as were two of my friends. I wasn't sure whether I was pleased they were there or not. I thought it might have been easier if they weren't.

When my turn came to speak, I pleaded guilty, just as my solicitor had advised me. Citing my youth and the fact that, while my record wasn't clean, I'd never been involved in anything so serious before, she asked for bail. She got it. To my astonishment, I was told I should go home to await sentencing.

The following week I was sentenced to two concurrent twelve-month supervision orders.

You might have thought that my first experience of being held in custody overnight would have been enough to make me consider where my life was heading, or at least to lie low for a while. Far from it. When I got home after my weekend inside, my mates were delighted to see me. Rather than thinking I was an idiot to have tried to rob an old lady's shop and got caught doing it, they treated me like I was a hero. They wanted to know all about my time in the cell. I bigged it up, making it sound more brutal than it was. When I relived my conversation with the chief superintendent, I gave myself lines I hadn't actually spoken.

'So I said to him, Chief Super, sir, you can kiss my fucking arse.'

My friends howled with laughter. I told the story so often, I started to believe it.

Even with my supervision orders, which meant that I had to see a youth justice worker twice a week, I didn't try to sort myself out. The youth justice worker assigned to me, Toni Dawodu, did her best. Looking back, I can see she really cared, but the walls were already up and she couldn't reach me. I continued to skip school. I was back with my mates, drinking every day and using all the drugs I could get hold of.

Pete's patience soon ran out. Whenever I was at home – to eat or to sleep – I ended up rowing with him or Mum. Pete wanted me to shape up or ship out. With no choice but to back up her husband, Mum threw me out of the house on several occasions. When that happened, I usually stayed with friends but one night, with nowhere to go, I ended up taking the bus to Heathrow, where I spent the night in the terminal, pretending I'd missed a flight. At least it was light and warm.

Mum and Pete were at the end of their tethers. I was so full of rage. I picked fights all the time. Once, when an argument escalated, I got right in Mum's face and screamed at her, calling her a hypocrite and blaming her for the way my life was turning out. Then I threatened to smash the house up. After that, faced with an ultimatum from Pete – sort me out or lose him and the two younger kids – Mum had no choice but to tell me to leave.

I went back to Heathrow. I spent two nights there this time, rummaging through the bins for food. The morning after the second night, I had a meeting with Toni, my youth justice worker. When I turned up looking dirty and dishevelled and very, very tired, of course she wanted to know what was going on. When I told her that Mum and Pete had kicked me out for good, Toni swung into action. She spent about an hour on the phone, calling round the local children's homes until she found a place for me. As I sat there and listened to Toni doing her best to find me somewhere to sleep that night, I wondered why she was even bothering. I was worthless. I should just kill myself.

'I've got you a bed,' Toni said at last.

I don't know if her own experiences made it a hard decision for Mum to agree that I be taken into care. Perhaps she hoped that the care system in England was different from the Nazareth home. What choice did she really have? Moving me out was the only way to keep the rest of the family together. Get rid of the most disruptive element.

Being in a children's home felt like one step down from prison. I had my own room and clean bedding but I hated it. I hated the rules and the restrictions and most of the other kids. Though we probably had a lot in common – most of them were the children of addicts and alcoholics like I was – I couldn't connect with them.

Despite being on curfew, I managed to escape most nights to buy drugs and alcohol. I always had a few cans stashed under the bed.

At that Stratford children's home, there was one care worker, a black guy, who reached out to me. One night, he came to find me and we had a long chat. He took the time to ask me about my life outside the home, about my siblings. About Pete. About Mum and her drinking. About Dad and his drugs. It was the most attention anyone had paid me for a long time and it felt good as I opened up. But after he left to get on with other stuff, the sadness of my life suddenly overwhelmed me. Alone in my room again, I couldn't sit with the strong emotions even that one conversation had brought up. I tucked into a few cans of beer, but this time the alcohol didn't make me feel better. It didn't even touch the sides. Making sure the door to my room was locked, I ripped open an empty can. I used it to cut my face, slicing all the way down both cheeks. It was instinctive. I thought that physical pain would distract me from the far worse pain I was feeling on the inside. As I sliced my skin, I felt euphoric. It was my first attempt at self-harm and it was a serious one.

Hearing me cry out, the care worker came back. He tried to make me open the door but I was paralysed with fear at what I'd done to myself. Eventually he kicked his way in. He probably saved my life.

I was taken to the local hospital and treated for my wounds. While I was there, I was assessed by a psychiatrist. Meanwhile the care worker pleaded with my probation team to get me much more support regarding my past. He could see I needed more than they were giving me. I needed understanding. Everyone seemed to agree. Promises were made that a proper plan would be put in place.

Soon afterwards, Mum agreed to have me home again.

12

Spring turned into summer. I was back home but I was spending a lot of time out. I was mostly hanging around with my old mate Ivan.

I knew Ivan from primary school and from the Ivybridge Estate, where his dad had a flat. Ivan was in the year above me at school. His parents, who were separated, were both Colombian. His mother was a deeply spiritual woman who took her Catholicism as seriously as my mum did hers. We had a lot in common.

For a while, Ivan and I didn't see much of each other when we went off to secondary school. He went to a comprehensive in Gunnersbury. Our paths just didn't cross. But we started hanging out again after meeting at a fight.

Ivan had a reputation to match mine. He was known for being short-tempered and hot-headed and also impressively hard. Turning up at the fight where we reconnected – I was there for the bloke Ivan intended to beat – I remember seeing Ivan doing stretching exercises to psych his opponent out. He might have looked like a twat, warming up as though he was about to take part in a professional boxing bout, but when he smashed the other guy in a matter of minutes, everyone had to agree that Ivan knew his stuff.

After I paid my respects and we were reacquainted, Ivan and I spent the summer together, raising hell. We were shoplifting, vandalizing stuff for the hell of it, breaking into cars. The local police were determined to nail us but we evaded them time and time again, until one night we were stopped and searched on suspicion of carrying drugs. There was no suspicion about it. Ivan and I both had drugs on us. We always did.

An officer called Danny Dandridge arrested Ivan while his female colleague dealt with me. I was drunk and high and I was determined I wasn't going in the cells that night so I fought the female officer like she was a man. She wasn't a soft opponent by any means but I managed to overcome her by pushing her hard and got away.

Apart from being a terrible thing to do, getting rough with that female officer was stupid. It wasn't as though the police didn't know who I was.

I handed myself in the next morning. I knew I was going to get nicked for what I'd done at some point, but I'd at least missed a night in the cells and I'd had time to call a local solicitor. Two of the officers came out to greet me in the station reception. They pushed my head down onto the counter, put me in handcuffs and read me my rights. They didn't treat me kindly. I didn't deserve it. I'd assaulted a woman. A woman trained to fight back, but nonetheless . . . My solicitor was outraged at the way the police dealt with me that day but there was nothing he could do but wait while I was taken back out to the cells. To the horror of the officers who'd arrested me, that afternoon I was bailed.

*

95

Out on bail on an assault charge, you would think I would have been a bit careful for a while. Far from it. The very next night I was out with Ivan again – he'd been bailed too – drinking and scoring more drugs. We thought we were like highwaymen. Evading the law. Living by our own rules. He had my back and I had his. We were the scourge of south-west London and we loved it.

September came around. A gang of us were in Twickenham one Saturday night. There was an event on at the stadium. Some friendly rugby match. Friendly on the pitch, but not so friendly off it. Twickenham was full of big blokes getting smashed in the pubs.

Me and Ivan were sitting on the bench near the crossroads, smoking and minding our own business, when one of those rugby blokes staggered past. I don't know what his problem was but he called Ivan a 'Paki'. Ivan let it ride but later on we encountered the same man again, on Cross Deep, standing outside a strip club, and for no apparent reason he gave Ivan a mouthful again.

This time, Ivan did not react so calmly. He threw a punch and a fight kicked off. The rugby fan was big but he was drunk and that made him unsteady. It was all going badly enough – the rugby fan was soon on the floor – when Ivan smashed a bottle and used it to stab the man straight in the face.

'Fuck's sake!'

I grabbed Ivan by the jacket and pulled him off, while he continued to throw punches. There was blood everywhere. All over the rugby fan. All over Ivan. All over me. I was sobering up quickly. Blood like that could only mean serious trouble, but getting Ivan out of that fight wasn't easy. When he was mad, he was unstoppable. He would have kept going until the bloke beneath him was dead.

'Fuck's sake, Ivan! Come on.'

We ran for it in different directions.

There were loads of witnesses. Cross Deep was on a corner where several roads met. Someone must be calling the police.

Not sure that I could run far and fast enough, I made the decision to climb a nearby tree. From there I watched what happened next. As I predicted, the police were there in a matter of minutes. They were all over the scene. My heart pounded so loud in my chest I was sure that they must be able to hear me. But no one looked up.

Slowly, I relaxed. The police were looking everywhere but overhead. I had two beers, some fags and some weed in my pockets. I calmly skinned up while the ambulance came to carry the rugby fan away and the police closed the road, taping off the crime scene and diverting the traffic elsewhere.

It was surreal. Not once did any of them glance in my direction. All I had to do was sit it out.

As it was, they picked up Ivan fairly quickly but I stayed up that tree for more than three hours, waiting for my moment to escape. My supplies ran out. I started to get cramp. It was getting cold. I was getting bored. I thought I might fall asleep and fall out of the tree sideways. But at last the police moved off, leaving behind a circle of police tape. I waited another five minutes to be sure, and then I slid down the tree, ready to make a dash for home.

That night I was wearing my favourite Schott jacket. I wouldn't have parted with the jacket lightly but I knew it was a liability now. Witnesses would have seen me wearing it. It was too distinctive. The police would be looking for it. While I was standing under the tree, a girl I vaguely knew walked by. I asked her if she would wear my jacket for me and give it back when we got to my place. I also figured that the police were looking for a bloke on his own, not someone just walking along with a girlfriend. She would be extra cover.

The girl agreed to help me out. I told her I needed to get a few things from the open-all-night shop. I walked into the shop and loaded up with fags and more booze. I felt like I needed a drink.

As I was coming out of the shop again, I walked straight into two officers. While I'd been sat up that tree, laughing at how oblivious the police were to my presence so close to them, they'd actually been watching me the whole time. They'd been biding their time as I had mine. They knew that eventually I would fall right into their hands. The precious Schott jacket was taken as evidence, as were the rest of my clothes. They were speckled in the rugby fan's blood. Dressed in another police jumpsuit, I spent the rest of the night in a cell and woke with a hangover that was to do with more than how much I'd been drinking.

Ivan and I were taken to different police stations so I didn't get to see him to work out some kind of story before we were interviewed. Once again, I was offered the services of a duty solicitor. I didn't want to use the solicitor I'd had before so I said yes to the offer. This time I got Samuel Larye.

Samuel Larye was black, younger than I expected, and unlike

any solicitor I'd had before. He seemed to understand that there might be something other than just being a psycho behind my bad behaviour.

He asked the kind of questions that none of the others had bothered to ask.

'Why are you so angry with the world?'

I trusted him at once and was eager to follow whatever advice he could give me. In the first instance, he advised me that I should simply answer 'no comment' in response to every question in the interview. He would be applying for bail.

I was being held in Richmond. Ivan was in Twickenham. We both went to Richmond Court on Monday morning. Samuel was there to represent us both. He told the judge everything he said he would. He talked about my home life and the lack of support I'd had since childhood. I thought it was going well. But when the question of bail came up, the victim's solicitor merely held up a picture of the victim's shattered face.

A picture is worth a thousand words, as they say. I saw the judge recoil from the sight of the victim's injuries.

We were charged with attempted murder. Bail was not granted. Not for Ivan and not for me. Samuel shut his eyes and shook his head. He knew what it meant. We were going to prison.

Ivan and I were taken back into the holding cells to wait for the van that would take us to Feltham Young Offenders Institution. Feltham! At last. All those fairy-tale threats of my childhood were coming true.

'We're going to fucking Feltham,' I said.

'Shut it, man.'

Ivan was gutted. He couldn't believe we were actually going away this time. I felt differently. I was excited.

I had no idea.

13

Ivan and I were together again in the back of the van that took us to Feltham. While he sat quietly and brooded, I was full of anticipation for the adventure ahead. Feltham. We were on our way. Forget what it would be like while we were in there. I had already skipped ahead in my mind and was imagining what it would be like when we came out of there. We would be legends. We would walk the streets of Isleworth like living gods.

Ivan had a more clear-eyed view. He shook his head.

'This is bad, man,' he told me. 'You don't know how bad it could be.'

While I was fantasizing about my triumphant return to Isleworth and the tattoos I would get to mark my time inside, Ivan was more concerned about how we were going to get out of this mess. He knew that a conviction for attempted murder could mean years inside, especially if all the blame landed on his shoulders. He asked me if I would stand by him and stick to the story that we attacked the rugby fan together, though we both knew that it was his decision to glass the bloke in the face that had got us where we were. I understood his strategy. Neither of us would say what really happened in the vain hope that if we ended up in front of a jury they wouldn't feel they could return a verdict on either of us 'beyond all reasonable doubt'.

'You know what to do?' Ivan asked.

'Of course, bro,' I told him. 'I ain't no grass.'

Ivan nodded.

We were in it together no matter what happened. Like two of the three musketeers.

After half an hour or so the prison van arrived at Feltham. It was a big place. Back then, the infamous young offenders institution was home to more than 750 kids aged between fifteen and twenty-one. We were taken to Lapwing, the wing where all new arrivals spent their first night. As we were led through the gates, I was still excited. I was finally inside the building that had loomed over my childhood like a twisted version of Willy Wonka's factory. I was going to turn this experience into a triumph.

Then it came to being checked in.

We signed papers. Photographs and fingerprints were taken. We were each handed a bag containing the things we would need for that night. There were prison clothes: a pale blue T-shirt, dark blue jogging bottoms and the kind of plimsolls you wore for PE at school. Then there was a toothbrush and other toiletries. Cheap-smelling soap. A toilet roll. After we'd been given all that we were taken aside to be searched.

'Strip down,' the prison guard told me.

I had anticipated this. Now I was a veteran of the police cells, I was used to being searched and knew I would have to hand over my personal belongings. I knew I wouldn't be allowed to keep my belt, for example. But I didn't expect what happened next.

'And your boxers,' said the guard.

'What?'

'Your boxers. Take your boxers off.'

'No way,' I protested. I'd never been asked to take my underwear off in the police cells.

'Come on,' said the guard. 'We haven't got all day.'

I thought about complaining again but something in the guard's eyes told me that he wouldn't take kindly to any mucking around. Instead, cursing the whole time, I took my boxers off and stood before the guard in the nude. I held my arms out and turned around slowly, like I was a fashion model.

'Have a good look,' I said sarcastically.

'I will,' said the guard, with equal sarcasm. 'Now squat.'

'Squat?'

'You know how to do it.'

'I know,' I said. 'But I ain't doing it.'

'We can do this the easy way or the hard way,' the guard said. 'Doesn't make a difference to me. I've got to be here all night and you're not going anywhere.'

He was pulling on a pair of rubber gloves and I had a sudden realization as to what the hard way might entail.

'Squat,' the guard suggested once more.

Feeling more humiliated than I had ever felt in my life so far, I bobbed down towards the floor and stayed there, looking like a dog taking a shit, until the guard was convinced that I wasn't trying to hide anything in my anus. Up until that point, I had never once considered hiding anything up there.

'Stand up,' he said after what felt like an age. An unnecessary age.

I stood up.

'Now you can put your clothes on.'

I snatched up my boxers. I walked away from that experience feeling violated. Perhaps this Feltham thing wasn't going to be such a laugh after all.

Check-in was over. We had been processed and prodded and duly humbled. At last we were taken to our cells for the night. As we'd been told, Lapwing was a soft introduction of sorts to prison life. A starter wing. All the wings at Feltham were more or less identical, with two floors of cells arranged in a V shape around an area used for serving meals and association (the one hour a day you were allowed out of your cell).

Ivan and I were put in separate cells. Mine didn't seem so bad. There was a single bed and a toilet behind a partition for privacy. I'd been praying for that much dignity at least, especially since the squatting experience. When I saw where I'd be sleeping, I decided that I could take it. If this was what my real cell was like, then fine.

The food was pretty good too. Though as I've said before, anything seemed good after what I got at home. That night it was pasta and vegetables or breaded chicken breast and mashed potato.

Lights out was called at around 10 p.m. I was too wired to sleep so I lay down on my bunk and listened to the sounds coming from the other cells on Lapwing. With my window slightly open, to get rid of the weird prison smell I wasn't yet used to, I could hear voices drifting through the night from the other wings as well. Laughter, shouting, whooping, people banging on the bars. Sounds of excitement, manic happiness, frustration and anger. It was like listening to the calls of animals in the darkness of a jungle night. Predators and prey. I knew which I was going to have to be if I wanted to survive.

14

The following day, Ivan and I were taken to the wing that would be our home for as long as we remained on remand at Feltham.

'You're going to Quail.'

It hadn't taken long for me to work out that Quail wing was regarded as the hardest remand wing in the whole institution. The prisoners on Lapwing were in for all sorts of offences. Some relatively minor. The prisoners on Quail were in a different league. You couldn't get onto Quail unless your offence was serious. Like life-threatening serious. Manslaughter. Attempted murder. Murder itself.

If Feltham was like a university for young offenders, the kids on Quail were the genius students. The A-graders. The cream of the bad crop.

After our first night, which I'd found boring in a single cell, I was happy to hear that on Quail I would have to share with a cellmate. I don't know how happy the man already in the cell was when he heard the same news.

Just like Lapwing, Quail was laid out on two levels. Ivan was taken to a cell on the far left upstairs. I was going to be in a cell nearer the entrance. I didn't realize at the time how much where your cell was on the wing dictated your quality of life. I'd soon find out.

Carrying all my stuff in a clear plastic bag, I followed the guard to my new room. He unlocked the door and quickly ushered me inside.

There was no ceremony. No introductions were made. This wasn't a weekend house party. The cell door closed behind me and I found myself standing between two beds, on one of which sprawled my new cellmate, a black guy with dreadlocks. He barely glanced up at me.

'I'm Michael,' I said.

'Dredd,' he told me, not taking his eyes off his newspaper.

I guessed that the bed he wasn't sprawling on must be mine. I put my bag on it and sat down. I tried to make conversation.

'You been here long?'

'Too long,' Dredd told me, but he didn't elaborate.

Dredd wasn't in a talkative mood that morning. I arranged what little stuff I had on my side of the room. I stuck a couple of photographs on the wall using toothpaste in lieu of Blu Tack. One was a picture of my little brother Justin. The other was of the whole family in Hayling Island in happier times. Without making it obvious, I tried to get the measure of Dredd. Did he look like he might warm to me or had he hated me on sight? If he'd hated me on sight, was he going to give me any trouble? Could I take him in a fight?

Probably not.

When Dredd finally stood up, I understood for the first time how big he really was. He towered over me. He was older too. Maybe already twenty. He stretched and yawned.

He held out his hand to me as though he'd decided it was time to be civil.

'All right?'

The cell Dredd and I were to share was relatively luxurious. There were two separate beds rather than bunk beds, meaning we didn't have to fight for the top bunk, and, as the cell had been built for two, the toilet had a door for privacy. As the prison population continued to grow, the prison authorities were sacrificing prisoner dignity to capacity. Single cells were being turned into doubles with bunk beds. These were cells with no door on the toilets; they hadn't needed it when the cells were used as singles. Prisoners in those cells kept their dignity by using towels as makeshift curtains.

For now, I was lucky. I had my own bed. I stashed most of my stuff underneath it. And now Dredd had acknowledged me. I gabbled on about how I'd come to be there. About the fight and Ivan with the bottle and hiding up a tree and being brought in.

'Your first time here?' Dredd asked me.

'Yes,' I told him.

'I thought so.'

To begin with, Dredd didn't really want to talk. He found my questions irritating. I asked him everything. I had no one else to ask. When do we get up? When do lights go out? When do we get to eat? Dredd responded with one-word answers or grunts. Or sometimes with a bitter laugh. Like when I asked him, when do we get to go to the gym? When do we get to go outside?

'Go outside? You're dreaming.'

Dredd explained to me that we were on twenty-three-hour lock-up. We'd be allowed out of our cells to get food and for an hour of recreation time. Only an hour. Feltham didn't have enough guards to cover anything longer. And that also meant that if anything happened, such as if people got into a fight, even that hour could be forfeited. Twenty-four hours in a cell. No wonder Ivan had been so upset. No wonder Dredd wasn't too pleased to be sharing his cell with a skinny white kid who couldn't stop talking. Eventually he told me that he was in for armed robbery. He'd been the getaway driver.

We lived in that cell. We ate, slept and shat in there. The only time we would be able to leave the block was to go to education, but education was a privilege you had to earn by staying out of trouble and being respectful to the guards. Very few prisoners got to go. Likewise the gym. And if I did get to the gym, a kid like me had little chance of getting onto the machines I actually wanted to use. Everyone wanted to pump their arms and their chests. The black guys hogged the upper-body machines, like they hogged the pool table in the recreation space.

I soon found out that during association the prisoners on Quail wing generally stuck with other prisoners of their own race. When he realized that he wasn't going to be able to shut me up, Dredd started to warm to me, but he was an exception. The black kids stuck with the black kids and the white kids stuck with the white. I had enemies before I even opened my mouth. It wasn't long before I met them.

At only just sixteen years old, I was a novelty on Quail. Most of the other kids were older, between eighteen and twenty-one. Every time I was out of my cell – getting food, stuff like that

– I could tell they were sizing me up. What's he in for? What's he done? They knew I'd done nothing good. That was a given. A prerequisite for ending up on Quail in the first place.

I had my hair cropped short. It was almost a skinhead. When I got it done, I liked to think it made me look hard but there was no doubt I was still a 'pretty little white boy' compared to my wing-mates. The inmates on Quail were mostly black. The wing's population was about 85 per cent Afro Caribbean. The way I looked was always going to give me trouble. Even when the other kids heard why I was there and associated me with Ivan, who had the advantage of being Colombian, they decided to push their luck.

It started in the shower on my second week. My mates on the street may have given me plenty of advice on how to conduct myself inside, but unfortunately none of them told me how to get a wash in peace. I quickly worked out for myself that nobody was getting naked in the showers. Everyone kept on their boxer shorts. It wasn't out of modesty, though. I didn't notice at first that, while people were washing, they were using their boxer shorts as a place to stash their valuables. But then I'd never thought that a bottle of shower gel would count as a valuable.

I was naive. I found myself a free showerhead and started to lather up under the tepid water. While I was washing my hair, I rested my shower gel on the pipes in front of me, when what I should have done is tucked the bottle down my pants, like they were a kangaroo pouch. It was a stupid mistake, but it was going to cause me more trouble down the line than I could begin to imagine right then.

I washed my hair. When I'd got the soap out of my eyes, I went to wash my body but soon found out my gel was gone. Someone actually nicked it while I was effectively blinded by suds.

'Who the fuck's got my gel?' I ask, thinking it must be a joke.

No one responds, though I can tell they're all eager to find out what happens next.

'Come on,' I say, still thinking it's a stupid prank. 'Stop messing around. Give me my gel back.'

No one hands the bottle over. I can feel everyone's eyes upon me and suddenly I realize this isn't an ordinary prank. I've been set up.

I'm wet and I'm cold and I just want to get out of there, but I know I've got to remember my mantra. *Anyone fucks with me, I'm fucking with them.* It isn't about the gel. I can get another shower gel from somewhere later on, but I know that if I walk away without it now I'm going to mark myself out as someone who can be messed with. Someone whose belongings are up for grabs. Next thing I know, whoever took my gel will be swiping the food from my breakfast tray. They'll be demanding my cigarettes. My radio. The little things that make a difference when you spend twenty-three hours a day in a cell. That shower gel is suddenly more important than an ounce of weed, a wrap of coke or any replica gun. I've got to get it back.

So I issue a challenge. In time-old Feltham fashion.

'Whoever's taken my shower gel,' I snarl, 'you can go and fuck your mum.'

It's a stupid insult. It doesn't make much sense. I don't even know who I'm supposed to be aiming it at. But it has the desired effect right away.

'Who you telling to go fuck your mum?'

My challenge is accepted.

His name is Pepsi. I've seen him around. He's one of the gang of black kids who hang out by the pool table during association, making sure the rest of us never get a turn. He steps out of the crowd of faces and I quickly size him up. I've heard his reputation. He's a nutter. He's not any bigger than me but I know he's strong and he's definitely not afraid of a fight. At twenty, he looks like a grown man. He's in for a proper violent robbery. The rumour is he left his victim brain damaged. And now he's starting on me. In the fucking shower.

This is my worst nightmare. A fight in the shower block with the wing's biggest psycho. The others are all whooping. They're ready for a show. To them this is the best thing that's happened all year.

'What did you fucking say?' Pepsi asks me again. He gets right in my face as he says it. He tilts his head so that the muscles in his neck stand out like ropes.

I can't back down now. I crush the nervous part of me deep inside and square up to him, even though I'm still only wearing my pants.

'I said that whoever took my shower gel should go and fuck his mother.'

Pepsi's eyes flash with incoherent rage.

'You fuck!'

He pulls back his fist.

I must be crazy but today I'm also lucky. I duck when Pepsi

swings at me and manage to land my own first punch well. It puts him on the back foot. He wasn't expecting that. I hit him again. He smacks me back. Messy but hard. Then we're both down. Scuffling on the wet floor. Rolling around. There's water everywhere. Soap. The floor's too slippery. I fear for my head. He tries to grab it so he can smash it against the tiles. I know I've got to keep on top of him. Whoever ends up on the bottom is dead.

Around us the other kids are cheering like they're watching a Vegas bout. But it's nastier than that. We're like two wild dogs fighting for survival. Blood flecks the white tiled floor. I don't know if it's his or mine. I'm crazed with panic and hitting blindly. I try to stand up but I can't get a grip. Pepsi roars. He gets me on my back again. I grab his chin and push his head away. Then I'm back on top of him. Punching, punching, right in the face. I punch and punch and punch. I think I hear his cheek crack. I keep punching.

'You fucking, fucking fuck . . .' I say.

By the time the guards pull us apart, I'm wild.

The guards took Pepsi and me straight to the governor. Later, when they marched me back to my cell, I knew everyone was talking about me in a different way. I tried to keep it dignified but inside my ego was punching the air. I'd done it. That motherfucker Pepsi knew not to fuck with me now. They all did. If there was going to be any comeback, I couldn't yet see it.

Alone with Dredd again, I felt I could relax. He gave a low whistle as I walked in.

'You crazy motherfucker.'

I knew he meant it as a term of respect.

I looked into the blurry mirror above the basin Dredd and I shared. My face was clear. Pepsi didn't manage to land a single punch on my head. He didn't do so well. He'd got a black eye. It was hard to see against the colour of his skin, but his eye was seriously bruised and swollen. He came off worse and everybody knew it.

After that day, it quietened down for a while. Me and Pepsi were questioned separately about what happened and I knew he answered the same way I did. We'd both played dumb, though the governor did his best to impress upon us that it would be better if we didn't. No one grasses anyone up in Feltham, even if the punishment is worse when you don't. Pepsi lost his gym privileges. I didn't have any privileges to give up and I wasn't likely to get them any time soon.

I didn't care. I was living off the story. When we were out of our cells during association, I heard people talking about me in tones of awe. Just like I always wanted. No one tried to cut in front of me in the queue for table football anymore. In our small world, I was suddenly a big man.

'He done Pepsi.'

'He's a fucking nutter.'

Fucking nutter? The highest compliment you can get.

People nodded at me now. I was getting the respect I wanted. All the same, under Dredd's guidance, I tried to act like it was no big deal. I didn't want to encourage anyone to think they needed to put me back in my place. Because maybe a little bit of me was starting to know that it couldn't stay this quiet forever. Somehow what I did to Pepsi had to come back and bite me in the arse.

I started to think maybe Pepsi was just waiting for his eye

to heal. Whenever we crossed paths, I read something in his expression. *Your time is gonna come, motherfucker.*

But when? When could it come? For twenty-three hours every day, Pepsi and I were locked apart. Me in my two-man cell with Dredd. Him? I didn't actually know where he was. We were kept well apart. When association came around, we were still under surveillance. There were guards everywhere. It wasn't easy for him to start something then. The guards knew to make sure we were never within hitting distance of each other. But I could feel his eyes on me when he thought I wasn't watching. How long could Pepsi wait for revenge?

15

Most of the kids on Quail found themselves there at the end of a long career of crime and violence that started when they were barely in their teens, but that wasn't always the case. Shortly after I arrived on the wing and had my run-in with Pepsi, another newcomer showed up. If I was unusual because of my age and colour, the new boy stuck out like the proverbial sore thumb.

I didn't get to know his name but I'll call him Jeremy, because that seems to fit the kind of person he was. He was about eighteen. Well-spoken. He probably came from a good family, had been to a good school. Maybe even a private school, judging by the way he carried himself when he first arrived. Whatever, if his life had gone the way it was supposed to, he definitely wouldn't have been in Feltham. He probably would have ended up in the Houses of Parliament.

I heard his story on the grapevine. Jeremy had never been in prison before, as if we couldn't guess. He had never even been in trouble with the police before. He'd ended up on the hardest ward in Britain's hardest young offenders institution through what you could only describe as sheer bad luck.

Jeremy was out clubbing in Slough with his girlfriend. The night was over and they were on their way home. Jeremy's

116

girlfriend stood by the door of the club while he went across the road to a phone box to call a cab. While he wasn't by her side, some dickhead came out of the club and started hassling her, touching her up. She yelled for help and when he realized what was going on, Jeremy raced back to defend her.

By the time he got to her, Jeremy's girlfriend was being hassled by three guys. Jeremy landed a punch on the ringleader. It was a good punch. Enough to make sure the dickhead knew to back right off. But what happened next would ruin Jeremy's life. Drunk as he was, the dickhead groper staggered backwards. He tripped over the curb, fell and hit his head. He died from the resulting head injury, and what had started as a fight the police probably wouldn't have bothered with suddenly became a murder enquiry.

Jeremy was tall and well-built, and that bought him a bit of time. Just as had happened with me when I arrived, there was a brief period of calm while the other guys on the wing tried to get the measure of him. After all, you didn't end up on Quail if you hadn't done something violent. So while everyone tried to work out where Jeremy fit on the scale of hard-core mentalists we were living among, he was relatively safe. But it didn't last long.

One thing Dredd had taught me was that getting and keeping your food long enough to eat it on Quail required serious tactics. When the doors to our cells were opened each mealtime, there would be a rush for the kitchen shutter in the middle of the wing. The black kids from the upstairs floor would always somehow be the first there, grabbing the best of everything and taking it back to their cells where they would eat it so quickly they'd be finished before the last of us was served. Then they'd lie in wait for the other kids on their floor to come back.

Trying to get back to your cell with a full tray of food was like being an antelope facing a run through a pride of hungry lions. I was lucky. Dredd and I were in a cell right next to where the food was set up. It was easy to get there and back without running into any trouble. Jeremy's cell was furthest away. He had no chance.

The first time it happened he might have protested, but Jeremy quickly learned that when one of the black guys upstairs told you he wanted your food, you let him have it.

Unfortunately, it set the pattern. Now that it had been established that Jeremy wasn't the kind to get into a fight, everyone started to have a go. Jeremy was probably just doing his best to stay out of trouble, hoping it would go well for him when he came to trial, but he set himself up for a nightmare of a time while he was waiting. Soon it wasn't just at mealtimes that he was getting picked on. In association he was getting shit from all quarters. He had no hope of getting on the pool table. Hardly any of us did. But he tried queuing for table football, only to be pulled off whenever he got on. The guards did nothing about it. They just watched from a distance. They'd only get involved if it got violent. It didn't bother them if Jeremy never got a game at all.

Little things, but little things can soon start to seem like a big deal when you're in a cell twenty-three hours a day. A match of table football seems like a fortnight-long holiday in Ibiza when there is literally nothing else to do. Jeremy started to shrink, and not just because he wasn't getting enough to eat.

He gave up on trying to get on the football table. He just sat in the corner, staring at the floor.

No one approached him. Much as some of us might have felt sorry for him, we all knew that it was a mistake to associate with someone who'd been marked out as weak. Weakness rubbed off on you; I knew that much.

Soon, Jeremy didn't even bother coming out of his cell at all. He confined himself to twenty-four-hour solitude. All he could do was count down the days until his trial and, hopefully, his release. At least he had a cell to himself.

One morning, soon after Jeremy gave up on leaving his cell except when he had to, he got out for good.

At seven o'clock the guards opened the doors to the cells on Quail as usual and we rushed to the canteen to get our breakfast. When I got to the food, they were still opening some of the doors further along the line. A guard got to Jeremy's door.

'Everybody back in your cells!' the shout went up. 'Back in your cells.'

'What the fuck?' said Dredd. 'We ain't had our breakfast.'

'You'll get it later. Back in your cells.'

Pissed off that breakfast had been cut short, we moved slowly at first but soon the guards were shoving us back behind closed doors and slamming shut the metal covers over our windows onto the wing. Whatever had happened, they were in a hurry to get us all tucked away again and make sure we couldn't see what they were up to. But the guard who closed in Dredd and me slammed the window shutter in our door so hard that, rather than close, it sprang open again so we could still look out.

While Dredd lounged on his bed and complained about being hungry, I pressed my face against the tiny gap to try to see what was going on outside. I saw the guards take a stretcher in the direction of Jeremy's cell. I saw them carry it back again moments later, loaded with a body shrouded in a blanket. Only one of Jeremy's feet was visible: pale and lifeless, like it was made of wax. I knew what it meant. Jeremy had found his way out and it was final.

It was the first time I'd seen a suicide, or at least the results of one. Though I didn't know Jeremy very well, it affected me more than I would have expected. I couldn't get the sight of that stretcher and the blanket-covered body out of my mind. In the cell with Dredd, I went over what I'd seen.

'Why did he do it?'

Dredd shook his head.

'Coward's way out, man.'

I just couldn't understand why Jeremy hadn't made it. I knew it wasn't exactly fun to be stuck on Quail on twenty-three-hour lockdown day after day, and he had it bad with the bullying, but not *that* bad, surely? Not bad enough that checking out of life altogether would seem like a better option than just keeping his head down and getting through? I bet that, if he'd got to his court date, he would have got a light sentence. He had no previous convictions. He acted in defence of his girlfriend. He didn't know that the bloke was so drunk he'd fall over. He didn't intend to kill him, just scare him off. It was an accident. Any jury would have seen that. But now he'd never find out and Jeremy's unlucky punch had claimed two victims.

No one knew for sure how Jeremy had killed himself – the

guards wouldn't tell us for fear of inspiring copycat attempts – but Dredd told me he thought it was most likely by hanging. Though it wasn't impossible, it was hard to get hold of enough drugs to take an overdose. If Jeremy had cut himself, I'd have seen more blood when he was carried away on that stretcher. Hanging was the obvious method.

I looked around the room.

'Yeah,' I said. 'But what would he use? He didn't have a rope and there's nothing to tie one to if he did.'

Dredd shook his head at my naivety. He was always shaking his head at me. 'He used a sheet or a blanket,' he said. 'And he tied it to the bars on the window.'

'But there's no drop.'

'You don't need a big drop,' Dredd told me.

I didn't get it. Patiently, Dredd explained how it was done. Jeremy would have made a rope out of a blanket by tearing it and twisting it, tied one end to the bars and another around his neck.

'Then he lies on the bed,' said Dredd. 'And rolls off. It's a short drop but if you get it right it still works. The rope jerks. You're gone.'

Dredd shook his head again. 'Coward's way out, though, man. Coward's way out.'

What happened to Jeremy really rattled me. It wasn't just that he'd got so desperate he killed himself. It was the similarities between his case and mine. Mine and Ivan's. Jeremy had not intended to kill his victim. It could have all been so different. Jeremy's victim might have fallen over and got straight back up and punched him back. What started out as a scuffle went massively wrong.

So far, our luck had gone the other way. The rugby fan was alive. When Ivan and I ran away from the scene, he looked a mess but he was still breathing. But what if he died before we got to court? What if those injuries Ivan had inflicted with the bottle had a delayed effect? It was still possible. Then our attempted murder charge would become a plain murder charge. My fantasy that I'd be out in three months when a jury couldn't decide whether Ivan or I had used the glass would be over. Luck. So much of the way life turned out was down to dumb old luck.

Samuel was still working to get us out. He saw me and Ivan on separate visits.

Once when he came to see me, he asked me again how I got so angry.

'My mum's a drunk. My dad's a druggie,' I explained all over again.

'But you can be better than that,' he said. 'You're no fool, Michael. You could have a different life. You shouldn't be here.' He did his best to break through the hard-nut act that I was clinging to harder than ever now that it felt as though it was the only thing keeping me from ending up like Jeremy.

Samuel knew from talking to both of us that I was not the one who'd stabbed the victim, but he also knew that I wasn't going to grass Ivan up and get myself off by telling the actual truth. Meanwhile, Ivan was planning to keep his mouth shut too.

Samuel despaired of us both but he understood the code of the streets and he didn't push me too hard to change my mind and save myself. Instead, he tried to persuade Ivan that he should plead guilty and leave me out of it. That was the honourable thing to do, surely? Plus, the evidence against Ivan was pretty over-whelming. There were plenty of witnesses who had seen how the fight really unfolded. Still, Ivan wanted to stick to the plan we'd come up with in the back of the van from Richmond Court to Feltham. We were two musketeers. All for one. I told Samuel that I would always have Ivan's back. Samuel rolled his eyes.

Besides, there might still be a miracle. Talking to Dredd and to the other prisoners in association, I'd come to hear about something called 'judge in chambers'. This was when a judge heard details of your case ahead of the trial and made a decision to call the trial off as a result. It was the criminal equivalent of winning the lottery. Other prisoners told me they'd seen it happen. You could be sitting in your cell at any time of the day or night and one of the guards would open up the door and tell you to pack your bags, you were going home. I dreamed it would happen to me.

Samuel sighed when I mentioned the idea to him. He re-iterated that so long as Ivan wouldn't confess and I wouldn't grass him up, he was going to have a hard time getting me off. Next to impossible.

16

Life on Quail had found a happy rhythm for me. Having started out finding me irritating, Dredd seemed to view me as a little brother now. We found ways to make those twenty-three hours of each day pass quickly. Dredd had a radio and he introduced me to loads of new music. We liked a lot of the same stuff, which was useful. We didn't argue over what we wanted to listen to. We told each other stupid jokes. We practised boxing moves. We shared newspapers.

There was other stuff to read too. I got a lot of letters while I was in prison, mostly from girls who thought it was glamorous to have a boyfriend on the inside awaiting trial. Some of them wrote several times a week. Dredd couldn't believe how many letters and cards I got. Even the guards seemed impressed. The old cliché about girls liking a bad boy was definitely true in my case.

'And all these girls think they're your girlfriend?' he marvelled.

'I never promised any of them anything,' I told him, full of secret pride that I was still on their minds.

Some of the letters were worthy of Mills & Boon. Dredd rolled about on his bunk, crying with laughter, when I read him juicy extracts in a high-pitched voice. He helped me to craft my responses. When the correspondence started to get properly hot, Dredd told me, 'Man, when I get out, you got to introduce me to some of these women.'

I got letters from people who weren't interested in 'banging my brains out' too. My mum's friend Mary often wrote, and when she did she would sometimes include a prayer card illustrated with a saint she thought appropriate to my predicament. One of my favourites was St Francis of Assisi. Mary said she prayed for me all the time. She even prayed for me at the famous grotto at Lourdes in France. She sent a photograph of her son in front of the Virgin Mary, adding his prayers to hers.

Every time I got one of Mary's letters, I rolled my eyes at her heartfelt sincerity and joked with Dredd that, if Mary really had a direct line to God, I'd have had my 'judge in chambers' moment weeks ago. Privately, I felt humbled every time I read her words, which were always so full of kindness and faith that deep down I was worth praying for. In my quieter moments, I didn't feel like I was. I couldn't believe that she was still bothering with me. I found myself thinking about the times she'd seen me hanging out in the square with my mates, drinking and smoking and generally causing trouble. She'd never walked on by or looked away. She always came over and said hello. Sometimes she even insisted that I let her hold my hands and pray for me, right there in front of my friends.

Though other lads my age might have laughed at Mary's concern for my spiritual welfare, I secretly found it comforting. She was like a second mother to me. She seemed to understand what I really needed. I kept the prayer cards and the picture she sent me of her son at Lourdes.

Meanwhile, Mum's communication was sporadic. It depended

on how she herself was doing. On the few times I saw her in the visiting room during that first stretch inside, she was grey-faced and puffy. It was obvious that she was going through a phase of drinking heavily again. She seemed to bring her unhappiness with her. I felt unsettled for ages after she'd gone. I didn't want to think about what was going on at home. I missed my siblings. I wondered what Pete had told them about me. None of them ever came to visit me. Mum was the only one.

Other people's visitors brought happier vibes. Like one of Dredd's old girlfriends, who smuggled in some weed in her mouth for his twenty-first birthday and passed it over to him with a tongue kiss. Dredd said he would share it with me. We had it together on his twenty-first, blowing the smoke out of the window so that, if a guard did walk in, we could at least pretend we weren't stoned. It was a warm evening and everyone was hanging out of their windows.

'Come on, Maisey! Share it around!' they yelled. My wing-mates were always passing drugs around. You could sometimes push it through to the next cell through the gaps in the walls around the plumbing. Inmates chiselled away the cement around the pipes to make the gaps bigger. To get stuff to people in the cells above or below, you could lean out of the window and send it down on lines made from thread unravelled from sheets and blankets. The guards knew, I'm sure, but they turned a blind eye. We were locked up for twenty-three hours a day. Drugs were the only thing that stopped a lot of the kids in there from turning homicidal. The guards were far happier to deal with stoned kids than murderously angry ones.

But on Dredd's twenty-first, he and I had the whole lot to ourselves and spent the evening side by side on our separate single beds, talking rubbish and laughing at pathetic jokes. He felt like my brother. I thought he would be someone I would always know.

'When we get out,' I told him, 'we're going to meet up and have the biggest night in the history of the world. We're going to be friends forever, right?'

'Yeah,' Dredd nodded.

I held out my fist to him. He smiled as he bumped his fist against mine.

'You're going to be out of here long before I am,' he said.

Before my trial with Ivan for attempted murder, I was due in court on another matter. I had to enter a plea regarding my assault on that female police officer back in August.

It's not exactly Chessington World of Adventures, but when you're in a cell for twenty-three hours a day even a trip to court starts to be something to look forward to. I said goodbye to Dredd. He wished me luck.

To be honest, I wasn't expecting that day in court to go my way and I was right. It didn't go well. Samuel did his best again. He told the judge he thought I was in danger stuck in among so many older kids on Quail, kids with records that would make Charles Bronson proud. I was young and I was stupid. I wasn't yet hardened like the rest of them. The judge didn't even look at me after Samuel finished talking and he delivered his decision. I could tell he didn't buy Samuel's picture of me as a good kid gone awry and who could blame him? Even by my own warped standards of the time, I knew getting physical with a woman was despicable. I was going straight back to Feltham.

My bid for freedom was over by lunchtime, but there were other Feltham inmates at the court that day and the bus wasn't going back until we were all ready. Someone's trial was over-running. It wasn't until hours later that we were back on the bus.

17

When finally we're on our way I'm still in a good sort of mood. A day in court is a day out for me. It's felt great to be out of my cell, to see other faces, to see people dressed in normal clothes, even if they weren't exactly friendly.

By the time we get to the Feltham gates it's dark. We check in at reception. One by one, we're counted back in and accompanied to our various wings and then to our cells. I don't recognize the guard who accompanies me and, given what happens next, vice versa must be true. He tells me that because it's so late, he's going to put me on the Quail dorm for the night. He doesn't have time to do anything else, he says. I don't care. It feels like relatively good news. Being in a cell on your own or with one other person gets tired after a while. In the dorm, I'll be with three other prisoners. I'm looking forward to the variety of three new people to get to know. I'm that desperate for novelty. Much as I love Dredd, I think I've heard all his stories at least twice by now.

Until the guard opens the door to the dorm and I recognize the first inmate. It's one of Pepsi's mates. One of the pool-table crowd. And there's another. And there, on the bed furthest from the door, is the man himself.

Fuck. Pepsi looks up from the paper he's reading. Our eyes meet.

What can I say? If I turn to the guard and tell him that me and Pepsi are supposed to be kept apart, will he do anything about it anyway? He's already told me it's too late for him to find me another bed for the night. I look from him to my old enemy and back again, hoping the guard will work it out for himself. He doesn't. Pepsi's face – now fully healed – widens into a grin.

'We're cool,' he says to me.

The guard is happy with that.

'Hurry up then.' He ushers me into the cell and closes the door behind me.

I am in the fucking lion's den.

But for the moment, nothing is happening.

'You can have this bed,' Pepsi says. It's the one closest to the toilet but right now I'm not complaining. I sit down. I think about taking off my trainers but decide against it. Not that I could run anywhere if I had to.

'Relax. We started off on the wrong foot,' Pepsi says to me. He can tell I'm not happy. 'Let's go from the beginning again. I want to know more about you, Michael Maisey.'

I'm on full alert. I don't trust this politeness. Adrenalin makes my heart beat faster, but I try to answer Pepsi as though we were meeting at a party. Like we could be friends.

'Where you from?'

I tell him.

'I know it. I'm sure we got people in common,' he nods. He seems pleased at the idea. 'But you're so young,' he tells me then. 'You don't look like a hard man. How'd you end up in here?'

In answer to his questions, I tell him more about my life outside. He tells me about his. He makes jokes. I make sure I laugh along with his two henchmen. They're relaxing on their beds. I go as far as leaning against the wall but I'm not lying down. Not yet.

'Where d'you learn to fight like that?' Pepsi asks.

It's the closest he's got to touching on our mutual history. I feel a shiver down my back. But I answer him by talking about the guys I know outside who taught me how to look after myself. He seems interested. Genuinely.

It gets later and later. I'm getting tired. I've been awake since six for my trip to the court. I know I shouldn't get too relaxed but for the moment everything seems to be going OK. I take off my trainers.

'That's right. Make yourself comfortable,' Pepsi observes.

Lights out at last. Pepsi bids me good night.

'Sweet dreams.'

I lie on the bed, eyes still wide open in the dark.

But I can't keep them open forever. My eyelids start to feel heavier by the second. *It's going to be OK, isn't it? It's got to be OK. He told me we were cool.*

When I wake, I am fighting for breath. For a second I don't even know where I am. There's something pressed over my face. I can't breathe, I can't see. All sound is muffled.

A punch to my stomach brings me back to the real world. Fuck. *Pepsi!*

He was only waiting until I fell asleep. Now there's a pillow over my face and blows landing all over my body. My lungs are burning as I desperately fight to get air. I try to push the pillow off. Someone grabs my arms and holds them out of the way. All three of them are on me!

Another punch. And another. The blows are coming faster and faster. The pillow shifts. I take a breath and chance a scream that's quickly silenced with a fist.

Back under again. The pillow pressed down harder. They're going to kill me. I've got to fight. I've got to fight. I kick out with my legs. Whoever had them is unbalanced. I get a chance to roll out of the way. The pillow's off my face for just a second. Another cry for help. Another punch. Blood's in my eyes but I catch a glimpse of Pepsi's through the dark red filter. There's nothing but hate in the way he's looking at me. He doesn't see me as human. He means to see me dead.

'Help.'

The word comes out in a bubble of blood.

'Help.'

A little louder this time but Pepsi forces it back into my throat.

'Shut up, you stupid white boy. Shut the fuck up.'

His hands are on my neck. The pounding of my heart is deafening in my head. All over the wing, other prisoners are waking up to the sound of my beating. They're banging mugs and plates against the bars. Joining in. Shouting. Egging Pepsi on. The guards have to be hearing it. They have to come soon. They have to!

The three of them keep punching. They're animals and I'm a piece of meat to them now.

It's like I float out of myself then and look down on my own body. The pillow has fallen to the floor. I see them laying into me. They're grunting like they're in the gym.

My cheeks are slick with my own gore. My nose is flattened on my face. I can't open my eyes. My body feels like a bag of broken bones. I know I'm not going to survive this. I can't. How can I? Three against one. My brain is replaying sixteen years on fast forward. Mum. My sister. Dad. I see Mary smiling at me in the darkness. Holding a hand out like one of the saints on her prayer cards. There's Samuel. He's leaning against the wall with his arms crossed like he does.

'Keep your head down,' he tells me.

Too late, Samuel. Too late.

Each punch comes in slow motion now. I feel the breeze of flying fists as they flash towards my face.

'Kill him!' someone's shouting. 'Fucking kill him!'

The shouting and banging have reached a crescendo. The alarm is tearing the air. But Pepsi and his friends are not going to stop now. They've got blood lust. I'm finished. I'm a statistic. This is my payback.

I whisper for my mother.

I think I'm already dead.

18

Apparently it was Dredd who raised the alarm. He was sitting by the open window of our cell, smoking, when he heard sounds of struggle. He knew at once that it was me. I hadn't come back to our cell after my trip to court. That meant I had to be in the dorm. In the dorm with Pepsi. Hearing my strangled cries for help, Dredd banged on his door to make sure the guards couldn't ignore me.

The guards reached the dorm just in time. I was already unconscious but still breathing. Pepsi and his mates were handcuffed and arrested for assault while I was taken for first aid. As I came round, my ribs hurt when I tried to breathe. My face was a mess. My mouth and nose were bloody. I could barely see out of my swollen eyes. But I was alive. I would be OK. Pepsi and his mates had not finished me.

I knew there was no hope that anyone would get done for that attack in the dorm. Like me and Ivan, Pepsi and his mates stuck by the code of *omertà*. None of them would speak to the police about what really went on. It didn't matter what the consequences were on the inside. They all knew that to break the code would have far worse consequences when they were back on the streets. They all played dumb to share the blame and make it impossible for any one of them to be charged for attempted murder, which was what it was. Had Dredd not come to my rescue, I would have died. I know it. But with no one, including me, willing to say how the fight started and who'd thrown the first punch, there was no real case. It was soon dropped.

I hadn't expected any justice – inside the walls of Feltham, it was like the Wild West – but that attack in the dorm room changed me. I suddenly understood why Jeremy had seen his future as so hopeless. There was no safety in that place, even if we were, in the eyes of the public, 'safely banged up'; I could have died just as easily as in a knife fight on the streets of Isleworth. The thought of spending the next few years watching my back made me pray harder than ever that by some miracle I would get off the attempted murder charge. Would Ivan really drag me all the way down with him? It was starting to look that way. Samuel continued to try to persuade Ivan to admit to the truth. I continued to say I wouldn't testify against him, though I was finally starting to realize how big a sacrifice I was going to have to make to stay true to my misplaced sense of loyalty.

At last our day in court came round. The night before, Ivan and I were moved from Quail onto the wing nearest the prison exit in preparation for an early start. We weren't in the same cell, but because he was in the one directly above mine we could talk to each other almost privately for the first time in ages, by shouting out to each other through our barred windows. I was doing exactly that, talking to Ivan about how we would handle the next day, when one of the guards walked in.

'Get your stuff together, Maisey,' he told me. 'I want to get you out of here before dinner time.'

Because I had my head half out of the window, I didn't really hear what he said to me. In any case, the idea that I would be going *home* that night was a long way from my mind. I didn't start putting my stuff together. I carried on talking to Ivan. The guard came back.

'Maisey, stop messing around. I want you out of here before we open the other cells for dinner.'

'What? Why?'

'You're going home, idiot.'

I just looked at him in disbelief. I'd had my 'judge in chambers' moment, the guard explained. Samuel had convinced the powers that be that there was overwhelming evidence of my innocence and it would be a waste of time to try me alongside Ivan. Since I was on remand for the attack on the rugby fan and not for assaulting the female police officer, I was free to go.

'You're kidding. How did he do that?'

'I don't know,' said the guard. 'All I know is I want you out of here. Get a bloody move on.'

I wanted to kiss him.

Now I realized that the guard wasn't taking the piss, I threw all my stuff together in seconds. I yelled up to Ivan.

'What's happening?' he asked.

'I'm fucking going home!' I shouted.

'You're what?'

'I'm going home.'

I left everything I didn't need for Ivan. My fags, my sugar, my matches, my radio. If he didn't want them, he'd be able to trade them for something else.

Ivan said he was pleased for me but we both knew what my freedom meant for him. He was standing trial alone because the evidence against him was overwhelming. There was no doubt in the judge's mind that, of the two of us who'd originally been arrested, only one was guilty of the attack. Ivan would not be coming home any time soon.

I wasn't the only one who hadn't expected me to be released that day. There was no one to meet me when I walked out of Feltham's gates wearing the clothes I'd been wearing when I went to Richmond Court three months before. I rang home but nobody answered. Mum and Pete were out at work. My sisters and brother were at school. I couldn't think of anyone else who might be willing to fetch me, so I waited for the bus. It was a sunny but chilly day; getting close to Christmas. Watching the world go by as the bus trundled towards Isleworth, I felt like I had been released into a film set. Everything seemed so colourful and busy after three months in the greyness of Quail wing.

One of the things I'd decided to bring home with me was a biography of Mike Tyson which I'd been reading at the time of my release. In it Tyson spoke about how he'd got a coach to help him change his life. High on my unexpected freedom, I decided that from now on I would try to be like Tyson. I had a chance at a better life.

When Mum and my siblings eventually got home that evening they were all shocked but pleased to see me. Pete was more reserved, though he warmed up when I assured him I'd learned my lesson and things would be different from now on.

'They'd better be,' he said.

I didn't backchat him. I was grateful to be with my family then. Especially with Christmas coming. The little ones were full of excitement about the season ahead. Having me back was going to make Christmas complete.

Tired from the surprising events of the day, I went to bed early, though I couldn't sleep. I lay on my back in my childhood room, taking in the familiar surroundings. I was warm. The sheets smelled good (the sheets in Feltham never smelled quite clean). It was quiet. Maybe it was too quiet. I'd got used to sleeping through any amount of noise.

I thought about Ivan, still waiting for his trial. I thought about Dredd. I never got to say goodbye to him. Not properly. That morning, when the guards came to move me to the holding wing, I'd still assumed I would be back. Ivan wasn't going to confess. I wasn't going to grass. I had never dared to hope that it would turn out like this. It was going to take a bit of getting used to, being on the outside again.

The day after I was released, I woke up feeling optimistic. I'd been doing some thinking about my next move. I knew I would struggle to get a normal job but it came to me that I could join the army instead. I felt sure they would accept me if I was willing to put my life on the line for them, despite my criminal record. I'd apply to an infantry unit.

I told Mum over breakfast.

'That's a great idea,' she said. I could tell that she was pleased and I was glad. I wanted to make her proud. So after breakfast, I caught the train into Victoria and went straight to the army careers office. By the time I walked in there, I was fully convinced that I was about to change my life.

In the interview with the careers advisor, I was open and honest. I didn't hold anything back. I explained that I'd just been released from prison and I told him about the charges.

'Stop right there, son,' he said when I mentioned the firearm.

'What?' I asked.

'I'm sorry but there's no chance you're getting in.'

My mouth dropped open. The careers advisor repeated his opinion. 'Not with a firearms charge. You're not right for us.'

I tried to plead my case but he just shook his head as I talked. Eventually, he stood up and physically escorted me to the door.

Even the army didn't want me now.

The following day was entirely different. I felt like I had nothing to get up for. It was late when I dragged myself out of bed. Mum was still home when I got up. I think she'd stayed off work because she was worried about me. She made me breakfast and asked what I was going to do that day. I told her I was going to go for a walk. She looked at me sceptically and asked me if I was going to meet my old friends while I was out.

'Only you know what will happen if you do,' she said. 'Stay away from them, Michael. They're bad news.'

I promised Mum I would. I could tell she didn't believe me but she had to let me go out. I was sixteen. She couldn't keep me in the house. Especially after I'd just spent three months locked up for twenty-three hours a day.

And at first, I did believe that I was just going to go for a walk. Get some fresh air. Get some exercise. But because I was walking around my old neighbourhood, of course it was just a matter of time before I bumped into one of my old mates.

I'd met Clinton back when I was hanging out with Jake all

those summers ago. Now he whacked me on the back with delight.

'Maisey! You're out. Let me get you a drink.'

I tried to tell him that I didn't want one but Clinton insisted.

'This is awesome,' he said. 'We thought you were going to be away for a very long time. We've got to celebrate. I want to hear all about it.'

Of course, it wasn't just going to be a single drink in a local pub. Clinton was working as a labourer so he had plenty of cash to treat me. He had drugs on him too. So I followed him down to a bench next to the river, which was where a lot of the old gang had taken to hanging out. Apparently, the parade of shops where we used to meet up was too busy with cops now.

Sitting on the riverside bench with Clinton on that bright December day, I started to get quietly stoned.

Soon, the news that I was out of prison had travelled all over the borough, and during the course of the afternoon Clinton and I were joined by a whole crowd of old friends. That bench by the river became the scene of a party. As guest of honour, I got the best of everything. No one would let me buy my own alcohol, cigarettes or gear. Everyone wanted to give me something, to pay their respects. In return, I told them all about Feltham. I still had scars on my face from the beating I'd suffered at the hands of Pepsi and his mates. I told the story of that night a dozen times. Each time, I fought harder and longer and came closer to death.

Some of the girls who'd written letters were there too, fawning over me and shooting daggers at each other. I looked forward to talking over their correspondence in private. But for that night, I was the man everyone wanted to be seen with. It was like being a superstar. I forgot all about Ivan. I didn't even know how his trial had gone. I forgot about Dredd. I forgot about the promises I'd made to Mum. And Pete. And my siblings.

Another drink. Another smoke. That's all I was interested in now.

I got home in the early hours, drunk and high. I staggered into the house, making a proper racket as I did so, not caring whether I woke anyone up. As it was, Mum was still awake, waiting with grim determination to find out if she'd been proved right. When she saw the state I was in, she went ballistic.

'I knew this would happen,' she said. 'I knew it!'

Her disappointment was huge and inside I felt guilt tug at my heart, but I didn't show it. Instead I walked by her and went upstairs. My attempt at starting again and staying on the straight and narrow was already over.

19

That second day of freedom set the tone. From then on I was up to my old tricks. I didn't even pretend that things were going to be different. I was enjoying the notoriety that being inside had brought me and I had more female attention than I could handle. Meanwhile, the young guys I hung out with treated me with even more respect than before. I felt like a king.

But the chief superintendent who'd tried to talk to me when I was taken in for armed robbery the previous year was right. Spending time in Feltham may have improved my image on the streets, but it wasn't going to help me get ahead in the real world. I didn't see the point in going back to school. I'd managed one GCSE, a D in English. It was the only exam I'd bothered to sit before the summer of craziness with Ivan. I couldn't find a job. Pete asked me to help out on his burger van. I think he hated the idea as much as I did but he was doing it for my mum, who hadn't quite given up on me yet. I went along a couple of times but didn't see the point.

I didn't care about rebuilding my life and carving out a real future. A lot of my old friends from school were doing apprenticeships and saving for their first cars and flats. All I cared about was having just enough money to get drunk and stoned with my mates and buy the stuff I wanted – clothes, trainers, music. I had an expensive lifestyle and no legal means of paying for it.

I wasn't going to risk holding up a shop again – too many places had CCTV now – but I still needed to get hold of stuff to sell. I'm not proud of this but I turned to burglary.

Just as when I first tried shoplifting, I targeted the leafy and affluent borough of Richmond. My time in Feltham had not mellowed my attitude towards the people who lived there and who seemed to have so much for no reason other than they'd been born lucky. Their parents weren't alkies and addicts like mine were. Everything came easy to them. I wanted what they had and saw no reason why I shouldn't redress the balance.

Far from the image of the burglar turning up in the middle of the night, I found it easier to turn the homes over during the day. I'd walk up and down the streets of Richmond looking for a likely easy target. It was always busy. There were always builders and delivery men coming and going so no one batted an eyelid when I walked by, looking like I had somewhere to go. When I saw a place that looked empty, I walked up the driveway and knocked on the door. If someone came to answer, I would say I was looking for Linda, just like in the old song Mum used to like. When the person who answered the door told me there was no one of that name in the house, I would say I must have got the wrong street and leave. However, if no one answered the front door, I headed around the back to see how I could get in.

You'd be amazed at how many people left their doors and windows wide open while they weren't at home, making it possible for me to walk or climb straight in and help myself. I don't know whether they were forgetful or trusting. Either way, they were unlucky.

Once inside, I'd look for things that were easy to walk away with. Cash, jewellery, stuff that was easy to carry and sell on. Laptops, cameras, stuff like that. Things I could stuff into my pockets or shove in a rucksack. I felt pretty invincible, convinced I had every angle covered and was brave enough to take on anything that came at me. This didn't change even when I had a few close escapes with people coming home while I was there. I had to jump out of first-floor windows a couple of times, as well as scrambling down drainpipes or across conservatory roofs.

I sometimes stole things to order. There were always people on the Ivybridge Estate who would buy stolen goods. The drug dealers would accept stuff for drugs too. Meanwhile, there was an Indian guy in Hounslow who would buy passports to be used in falsifying ID. Ivan had told me about him. I could get very good money for a passport. Pete spent all day on that burger van trying to earn what I could make in a few minutes going through the drawers in a stranger's dressing table. I thought he was a mug. I thought anyone who had a job was a mug, especially when I really hit the jackpot. Like the time I opened a wardrobe and found a handbag stuffed with thousands in crisp new notes. It actually made me wonder what the house owner was doing to be keeping so much cash. The only people I knew who had cash like that were drug dealers. I took the money and got out of there as quickly as

I could. I wasn't going to wait around to find out if my hunch was right.

Given that I was breaking the law pretty much every hour I was awake, it wasn't long before I came to the attention of the police again.

This time it was personal. There were people who were pretty angry that I was out of Feltham, regardless of what the legal situation was. Whenever the police pulled over anyone I knew, the first question they asked was, 'Where's that little shit Maisey?' They wanted to see me back inside and were just waiting for an excuse to pick me up. Like an idiot, I gave them that excuse. I hadn't been home long before the police had me in their sights for a number of offences.

They came for me one morning. Like the time the flying squad turned up to arrest me for the armed robbery, they arrived early while I was still in bed. *Luckily* for me this time. Mum answered the door like before but now she knew what she had to do. She didn't just stand aside and stare in bewildered panic. She told the police that I wasn't home.

'I don't know where he is,' she said.

They didn't believe her but when they said they wanted to come in and search the house anyway, she asked them whether they had a warrant. They didn't.

'Then you're not coming in. End of story.'

Mum sent them away. They were gone before I'd even woken up.

Mum came upstairs. She was furious.

'What the fuck have you done this time, Michael?'

For the moment I was safe, but Mum and I both knew

that not having a warrant wouldn't hold the police at bay for long.

'If you don't want to go back inside, we've got to get you away from here,' she said. She didn't just mean that I should go make myself scarce for a couple of days this time.

'Pack your stuff,' she said. 'You're going to Ireland.'

As soon as the shops were open, Mum went to the travel agency on the high street and bought me a one-way air ticket to Belfast. It cost her 150 quid, which was more than she could afford, given how much she was still spending on booze, but she decided it was a price worth paying to keep me out of prison.

'Who am I going to stay with?' I asked.

There was only one person Mum knew in Belfast who had room for me.

My old Uncle Tommy.

By the end of that day I was in Belfast. It was my first time ever on a plane and as we crossed the Irish Sea I had a moment of reflection. I'd been stuck in a few square miles for most of my life. There was a big world out there I'd yet to discover. I could go anywhere. Maybe this was the moment everything changed for the better.

Tommy was going to meet me at the airport. Walking into the arrivals hall, I scanned the crowd for a familiar face. It was more than a decade since I'd last seen my uncle. A lot had changed since then. As a four-year-old, I'd been terrified of the big man he was to me. All those nights I'd lain awake, waiting for him to creep into my bedroom. Landing in Belfast as a sixteen-year-old fleeing the police, I couldn't see anyone in that arrivals hall who would have the power to intimidate me.

There was, however, a shambling drunk heading in my direction.

Uncle Tommy was absolutely shit-faced. When he saw me he flung his arms around me, like I was his best nephew and he was my favourite uncle. I pushed him upright and away from me, recoiling from the unwashed smell of his dirty clothes. He was in no state to drive me anywhere so I was almost relieved when he said, 'C'mon. We're getting the bus.'

After he'd left our flat on the Ivybridge Estate, Tommy had gone back to Belfast and, on paper, for a while he seemed to be building himself a pretty good life. He got married and had three children of his own. However, Tommy's wife had recently kicked him out and was refusing to let him see the kids. He was living on his own in a flat.

Tommy led me to the bus stop, weaving and bouncing off walls and other obstacles on his way. He was so drunk he could hardly see. It got worse. While we waited for the bus, with a big queue of other people who just wanted to get home, Tommy peeled away from me to take a piss against a wall. He had no sense of where he was and chose the exact wrong spot – uphill from where we'd been waiting. His urine ran back downhill past the waiting passengers, who held their noses and turned their faces away in disgust.

Tommy was a shambles. Of course, his flat was a mess and dirty too. He wasn't working. Hadn't been for a while. He spent his days drinking or passed out on the sofa. When we got back to his flat from the airport, the first thing he did was get another beer out of the filthy fridge. He lay down on the sofa and was asleep before he finished drinking it, leaving me to work out for myself where I was supposed to set my things up.

Tommy was obviously not doing well but, all the same, when he was awake he tried to impress me with his stories of the IRA. One day he took me to the Falls Road where we bought Republican memorabilia. He took me drinking in Republican pubs where a kid with a skinhead and an English accent should have been in fear of his life. In the Catholic part of Belfast, any young English man could be mistaken for a hated British soldier. The rest of the time we drank at home, listening to his beloved Wolfe Tones until one of us passed out.

I stayed with Uncle Tommy for a month. I think I must have suppressed most of my memories of his time in London because, for the most part, while I thought he was pathetic, I enjoyed hanging out with him. It was easier to be in his flat than at home with Mum and Pete. He didn't have a go at me for not finding a job. He didn't care if I got drunk night after night.

Then, one night, it happened. He tried it on. I was sleeping on the sofa when Tommy came in from a night in the pub. He'd been drinking so much, he could hardly walk. As he lay down on the sofa next to me and his arm snaked around my middle, just like it used to do when I was small, I had a flash-back. I felt a lurch in my stomach as I smelled his breath in my face.

'Fuck you!'

I wasn't a little kid anymore. I jumped up and pushed Tommy to the floor. Even if I hadn't taken him by surprise, it would have been easy.

'Please don't hit me, Mikey. Come on, Mikey. Don't hit your uncle. I'm sorry, Mikey.'

I hated it when he called me Mikey.

Tommy begged my forgiveness as I towered over him, my hand clenched into a fist, threatening to smash his face in. I didn't need to. He crawled away from me like a pathetic crab. I covered my own face with my hands as the memories of those nights in the Ivybridge flat came flooding over me. I never, ever wanted to be that vulnerable again.

I knew I couldn't stay with Tommy a day longer. I could not continue to pretend that what had happened all those years ago hadn't affected me. The next day I called Mum and told her that I needed to move on. I didn't tell her why; I didn't think for a moment she'd believe me. Instead I said that I was bored in Belfast and I wanted to join my friend Tom – a friend from my days with the replica gun – who had been sent to Shannon by his own family, who also hoped that getting him away from his old mates would keep him out of trouble.

Mum agreed to the plan. She would pay for me to get there. Uncle Tommy could have driven me but he said he couldn't cross the border. He took me only as far as he could. I was glad. I didn't want to spend any more time with him than I had to. Beggars can't be choosers but I would rather have crawled to Shannon than take a road trip there with my abuser.

Tommy took me to a train station. We said a quick goodbye

before he got back into the car. He tried to hug me. I wouldn't have it. Then he took off so fast his wheels were smoking. It was to be the last time I ever saw him.

I stayed in Shannon for a while but it was no good. I enjoyed being with my old London mate Tom, rather than my uncle, but I had no work, very little money and I was bored. The novelty of being somewhere where no one knew who I was or about my history was wearing off. I missed the respect and street cred I had in Isleworth. Eventually, I decided that going back home and facing arrest had to be better than dying of boredom in Ireland. I spoke to Mum about it at length. She agreed. She encouraged me to come home and do the right thing. So I went back to London in the summer of 1999 and handed myself in for the offences that the police had come to arrest me for the day I fled. I was charged with eight. Two counts of burglary with intent, two counts of burglary and theft, one count of handling stolen goods, two counts of damage to property, and one count of taking a motor vehicle without consent. The coppers who had been trying to nail me for months had me at last.

Before I knew it, I was back in Feltham for a second time in eighteen months.

This time, I was not so excited at the prospect of two to three months of incarceration while waiting for my trial date. I wasn't on Quail, but though the wing was different the routine was exactly the same. Twenty-three-hour bang-up.

At first I was in a single cell. After the near-death experience I'd had with Pepsi and his mates during my first stint inside, I was determined not to find myself in that situation again, so

I insisted that I got a cell to myself. However, after a while, I got bored of my own company. The only time I saw my wing-mates was at mealtimes or during association. While we could also talk to each other through our cell windows, it wasn't the same as having someone right there and I was getting desperately lonely. I lasted three weeks. The only problem was, if I asked to be moved back into a double cell, I wouldn't be able to choose who to share with. I'd been lucky with Dredd. I knew that now.

However, during association I'd found out that one of my old mates from Isleworth – Mason – was on the same wing awaiting trial. He was in for a variety of crimes like theft and burglary that he'd committed to fund his crack and heroin habit. Like me, he was in a single cell and, like me, he hated spending twenty-three hours a day on his own. So we hatched a plan. We told the guards that we were cousins, knowing that the prison had a policy of housing relatives together where possible. They took us at our word and put us in a double.

After that, prison life was much more interesting. Mason and I spent hours talking about life in Isleworth, our friends in common and what we were going to do when we got out. We played cards for matches, mostly blackjack but sometimes our own invented games. We got on really well. I don't remember us ever having an argument.

We took it in turns to buy batteries for our crummy little radio. Since it was on from the moment we woke up to the moment we went to sleep, that radio seemed to need new batteries every week. We were lucky in that respect too. Our cell was right next to where the canteen set up at mealtimes.

That meant we got the best of the food and we got to hold on to it. It also meant we got the best of the 'luxuries' on offer at the canteen once a week.

We prisoners didn't have any money but we each had a sort of account to which our friends and families could contribute via postal order. Occasionally, Mum would put some money in. So would some of the girls who liked to think they were in a relationship with a bad boy. When I had cash, I would spend it on those all-important batteries, on matches, cigarettes and newspapers. I'd also buy Pot Noodles and Maryland Cookies, which were considered a real treat.

Sharing a cell with Mason made my second time in Feltham way easier than the first. Being able to talk to him made me forget that I never had any visitors. Not even Mum, this time. By pretending to be cousins, we'd worked out a way to survive.

Other inmates had their own strategies for getting by. There was a kid called Graham who went to the extreme. He pretended to be a Jamaican. Graham was an obvious target for bullying. He was white and he had a lisp. So he affected a full-on Jamaican accent. It cracked us all up. Still, it seemed to work for him, though perhaps not in the way he had hoped. There was no way Graham could pass as a Yardie. He could, however, pass as someone who was completely fucked in the head and therefore not to be messed with. I think the bullies avoided him because of that.

When I saw Graham again years later, at a probation office, he was still putting the accent on.

So, it was my second time in Feltham. I stuck it out. I kept my nose clean. I even managed to get a couple of privileges

– a single game of football and a visit to the gym. Then I got released. I went home. It was just before Christmas 1999. Once again, I was determined not to go back inside and yet, in reality, I had very little desire to make the changes I needed to ensure I stayed free.

I was on a path of self-destruction.

20

Now that I'd done two stints inside, my chances of leading anything like a normal life were even lower than before. I couldn't persuade anyone to give me a job – not that I really wanted one. I was back home living with Mum and Pete. Pete was barely speaking to me. The tension between us was pushing Mum to drink more than ever. I was only happy when I was with my mates. At least it felt like they were willing to give me another chance.

It was about this time that I met a dealer called Greg. He was in his thirties. He started coming round to where I was hanging out with my friends on the old Ivybridge Estate, offering us drugs. Not to use, but to sell. He didn't ask for anything upfront. He just gave us what he had and told us to pay him when we'd sold it. I had no money. Greg was offering free supplies that I could turn into cash. It seemed like a win-win situation.

Unfortunately, I turned out to be a terrible drug dealer. I took the stuff from Greg with every intention of selling it on and splitting the profits. In reality, when I had those drugs in my possession there was no chance that I would let them go. I'd get drunk and break into my supplies, with the intention of taking 'just a little bit'. I was like a fat chef, sampling everything that went through the kitchen. Taking first just the smallest nibble, then a teaspoon, then stuffing my face.

It had been several years since Jake had introduced me to heroin in Mum and Pete's garden shed. I'd somehow managed to stay away from the stuff since then. Likewise, I hadn't been doing much crack. But now I had access to a ready supply. Crack and heroin. The evil twins. One to lift me up and one to bring me back down again.

I was quickly using more than I was selling. Just as Jake had warned me, heroin was not a drug to take lightly. It was just a matter of days before heroin utterly dominated my thoughts.

Greg didn't care what happened to the drugs, so long as he got paid. Whether I was selling the goods or using them myself didn't matter to him so long as his expenses were met. That meant I had to find the money to cover what he'd given me. By now I'd been kicked out of home. I wasn't working. I was sleeping on friends' sofas. My only option was to start with the burglaries in Richmond again. I stole stuff to sell to get the money to buy drugs. I was high every day. I'd graduated from small amounts of crack to whole ounces and I was managing my comedown with heroin. It felt horrible waking up and needing that fix to feel good, but at the same time it was so satisfying once I got it into my system. I would swing between desperately wanting to give it all up to loving it once I'd had the hit. Really loving it.

Before I knew it, I was in a cycle I had no chance of breaking. Robbing from the rich to feed *poor me*. Crime, drugs, crime, drugs, crime. I got desperate. I got sloppy. The police caught up with me.

On 13 August 2000, I went back to Feltham for a third time.

*

To be back in Feltham was bad enough. To be back in Feltham as a full-blown heroin addict was worse than I had ever imagined possible. This time, I was put on Wren – the hospital wing. It sounds specialized, like it might be full of proper beds and resuscitation equipment, but in reality it was just like all the other wings except that a doctor visited more often. Only not that often.

Obviously, there was no way I could keep up my drug habit now that I was back inside and that was going to be a problem. A doctor prescribed methadone to keep me going for a while until I could detox. I was offered a choice of detox methods. I didn't feel anywhere near ready for a detox but it was made clear to me that I was going to have to give it a try. I got the sense that, if I did, it would make it easier for me to get parole, apart from anything else.

There were two options. A fourteen-day detox or one that lasted just seven days. I knew it was going to be painful which-ever method I chose, so I simply went for the one that promised the quickest results. It was essentially cold turkey. A doctor talked me through the process and then I was given a handful of medication before being sent back to my cell to let nature take its course.

Alone in my cell again, I lay down on the bed, feeling pretty confident that the next few days should be simple enough. All I had to do was *not* take drugs, sit tight and ride out a few cravings, job done. I didn't think I'd been taking heroin for long enough to have a proper *Trainspotting*-style comedown. I wasn't an addict like the ones you saw on TV. I was going to be fine.

And for a little while I was. I did what I usually did to pass the time. I read the papers. I listened to the radio. I listened to the sound of other kids on the wing. There was one kid who wouldn't stop screaming. He was begging for more drugs or to be put out of his misery. I thought he sounded pathetic. I wasn't going to be like that. No way.

A guard looked in on me from time to time. When I saw his face appear at the hatch, I gave him the thumbs up. It was going OK. I wondered how long I'd been detoxing. Ten hours? Twelve? I looked at the clock on my radio. Half that time. Why did time feel like it was passing so slowly?

Not long after, I felt a twitch start up in my eyelid. I felt tired and yet I didn't feel sleepy. I longed for night to come, thinking that sleeping would make the hours pass more quickly. By the time I woke up the next morning, I would be a third of the way through the worst.

Soon I couldn't concentrate enough to read. I counted the bars on the window. I counted the tiles on the floor. I kept having to start again. I closed my eyes and tried to count sheep. I couldn't even picture a sheep let alone start counting them. Down the corridor, the kid I didn't know was still screaming. I was still sure it wasn't going to be that bad. In three days the drugs would have cleared my system. Wasn't that what I'd been told? Anyone can last three days. Not having drugs couldn't kill you like having drugs might. You couldn't die from not doing something. You couldn't overdose on fuck all. And I was detoxing from heroin, not stopping chemo. This was good for me.

I looked at the clock on the radio again. Only thirty minutes? That couldn't be right. I was starting to feel hot. A sheen of sweat covered my top lip. When I tasted it, it didn't taste good.

It was metallic, like I was sweating blood. I jumped up and looked at myself in the mirror, suddenly needing to be sure that wasn't actually what was happening.

No. My face looked normal. I grimaced at myself. My teeth were all still there. They weren't loose, though that's how they felt. My eyes, too, looked OK, despite feeling like they were boiling. I was fine. I was going to be fine. It was hot in the cell. I was itching because the blankets were scratchy. I lay down on the bed. Closed my red-hot eyes. Tried to sleep. Heard someone trying to get my attention.

'Wake up.'

I sat up. Who was talking to me?

'Wake up, you little shit.'

What?

I jumped up and away from what seemed like the source of the voice.

There was nobody in the room and yet I heard them clear as a bell.

'You're not sleeping now.'

21

So this is it. This is how I'm going to die.

On my own. In a cell. With a dirty sheet wrapped around my neck.

As soon as the guard closes the door behind him after the hourly check, I get to work. Ripping the sheet into shreds with a strength I didn't think I had anymore. Getting them to the right size to do the job properly. Quickly. Before I change my mind.

I thought I could do this but it turns out I can't. I can't take the pain and I can't take the nightmares. Without the drugs, every time I close my eyes I can see them leaning over me, hear them talking about me, telling each other what they're going to do to me while I'm asleep. When I open my eyes, I can still hear them talking and I can feel the things they've put inside me crawling all over me, eating their way out. I can see them moving under my skin. I've got blood under my fingernails from scratching but nothing is going to stop them. Nothing except this. I want to close my eyes one last time and not see anything ever again. Never hear anything. Never feel anything. I want this to be done.

I know this works. I can't get out of this room by walking. I can't jump. I've got no pills to take. I can't cut myself. But they've left me one escape. The sheet is a rope now. Like Dredd said, one end tied around the bars on the window will do it. The bars won't let me down. They're designed to keep me in after all. They're not going anywhere. They're going to do their job.

Tying the sheet around one, I pull hard on the knot to make sure it will hold. The thin cotton tautens around the metal so that the only way to get it off will be with a knife. Same around my neck and . . .

Is this the proper knot? I've never seen it done in real life. I'm guessing. I don't want to get it wrong. I don't want to fuck even this up. When I lean back, it has to get tighter fast so I don't get a chance to think about it. I don't want to have time to chicken out.

One end around the window bars. The other round my neck. This should be simple. Down the corridor, someone is shouting. It's a distraction for the guards, giving me time to get it right. I think about the posh kid on Quail wing. The one who topped himself. How did he position himself? Where was the knot? I know there's a way to do it so that, after I let go, it'll happen before I know it.

I kneel in the middle of the floor to say one last prayer, looking like the dog that used to live at the end of our street. Chained by the neck, day in, day out. Barking, barking, barking, going mad. What was he even born for? What was I even born for? Who gives a shit anymore?

I say my goodbyes though no one will hear them. I say my sorrys too. Sorry, Mum, that you're going to have to see me on a slab. Sorry, Pete, that I couldn't be a better stepson. Sorry, Dad, that I couldn't be better than you were. Sorry, Mary. You believed in me but it turns out that I am a piece of shit and now I'm going to die like one. I'm going to die with a sheet wrapped round my neck, stinking of piss, sweat and tears. Looking like the loser I am.

I'm sorry, I'm sorry, I'm sorry.

Do it. Do it, you fucking coward.

The voices want one last say.

Get on with it.

I get up from the floor then I get on the bed and lie down. I just have to roll off the side. The drop doesn't need to be big. It just needs to be definite. Holding the sheet rope, I get into position and then I let go and I roll and the bed disappears from under me and . . .

22

I got the knot perfect. As I rolled off the bed it tightened at once, jerking my head back harder than I ever expected. It knocked the breath out of me and squeezed my windpipe so hard I couldn't take another. Instinctively, my hands went to my neck and I tried to loosen the noose. No chance. It was too good. For once I'd actually got something right.

Jesus!

Nothing to do but let it happen. But fuck, I didn't want it to happen. I scrabbled to free myself. I was on my back. My heels slid along the floor. I couldn't get my feet under me to lift me up and out of danger. Darkness started to creep in at the edges of my vision. Of all the mistakes I'd ever made, this one was the fucking worst.

I couldn't loosen the noose. I couldn't cry out. I was fucked. So absolutely fucked. I could only go through with it. As I realized that, I felt a sense of peace. I blacked out and waited to die.

But I didn't die.

I don't know how long I was out for, but when I came round it was to find that someone was pressing hard on my chest, trying to resuscitate me. I could hear shouting. Blurred silhouettes loomed over me. The metal door kept crashing against the wall as people rushed in and out of my cell. The rope was gone from around my neck. I was back on the bed. I spluttered into life.

'Thank fuck,' someone said.

'Stupid fucking idiot,' said someone else.

'Who last looked in on him?'

'He was doing OK. He was asleep.'

'Fuck's sake.'

The guards argued over my head as to whose fault it was that I had nearly managed to kill myself. There was no pretence that they were really worried for my welfare. They were much more worried about how they were going to explain what had gone on to their superiors.

'At least he's not dead.'

I'd saved them a lot of paperwork.

Flat out on that bed, looking at the ceiling that I had thought would be the last thing I ever saw, I started to cry. What I wanted, what I needed, was someone to hold me. Instead the guards searched my room, possibly looking for anything else that might get them into trouble. Even an unsuccessful suicide attempt was bad news on anybody's watch.

After I tried to hang myself, I was moved to another cell. It was a 'padded cell', carefully stripped of anything a prisoner could use to off himself. There was a window but it was specially reinforced so there were no bars to anchor a noose. No sharp edges. No mirror. Not even a proper blanket. Instead there was a plastic blanket like the one I'd been given on my first night in police custody, back when I was fifteen. I couldn't wrap it around my neck. It wouldn't even wrap around my body like a proper blanket should. I never felt warm enough when I tried

163

to sleep. Not that it was easy to sleep when someone was checking up on me every half an hour, opening the hatch in the door and shining a light straight into my face. I might have dodged death but it was still like being inside my own nightmare.

Meanwhile, I continued to detox. More gently this time. A new doctor prescribed slower withdrawal to avoid the kind of episode that led to my trying to die. It was still miserable. I still heard the voices. I was tired and distressed. I still wanted out but had no means of achieving it. Being in the padded cell kept me alive.

A week after my suicide attempt, I had a visitor. I walked into the visiting room to see Mum sitting at the table. She'd been told what had happened, of course. Her face was etched with worry as she watched me sit down opposite her. She studied me to see that I was OK. I knew I didn't look it. I'd lost weight. I was grey-faced. My arms and neck were covered in scratch marks from trying to get rid of the incessant itching that came with withdrawal. Mum did her best to hide it, but I could see how shocked she was in the way her smile didn't reach her eyes.

For a little while we chatted about everything and nothing. She filled me in on the news from home. She told me what Maria was up to, how Justin and Sophie were getting on at school. What Pete was doing. The gossip from Mary, who, naturally, sent her love and said she was praying for me every day. Mary would never give up on me. Then Mum told me some news of her own.

'You might have noticed there's something different about me,' she said.

It was true that, even though Mum looked worried, she didn't look anywhere near as bad as she usually did. Her face looked sharper somehow. Not so puffy.

'It's because I'm getting sober.'

'What do you mean?' I asked. The detox was making me slow.

'I mean, I've stopped drinking. I had to. It was ruining my life.'

After an adult life spent getting drunk pretty much every day, Mum had finally decided that she was an alcoholic. 'I've joined a twelve-step programme,' she told me. 'And I'm going to meetings. It's really helping, Michael. I haven't had a drink in a month. When you get out of here, you should try it. You can come with me. I'll take you along.'

'What are you talking about?' I asked.

She fixed me with a steady gaze. 'I'm an alcoholic, Michael. I finally realized I need to do something about it. I didn't tell you what I was doing before because I didn't want to jinx it, but it's working for me and it could work for you too. When you get out of here, I'll do everything I can to help you start over. Would you like that?'

All my life, all I'd ever wanted was to feel unconditionally loved and supported by my mum. All my life, until this moment, she'd been distracted. By Dad, by Pete, by my siblings, but most of all by alcohol. I didn't know what to say. Could I believe what she was telling me over that bare tabletop in a prison visiting room? I wanted to.

Just like every other public space within the prison, the visitor room was somewhere you were on show to your fellow prisoners and guards. Any sign of weakness, like getting upset when you saw a member of your family you so badly missed, would be taken advantage of later. You could be sure of that. It was important to keep your mask on at all times. You couldn't break down. You couldn't risk it. But that day I did.

When Mum told me that she was getting sober and she wanted to help me to do the same, I just couldn't hold the tears in. I wanted to be a little kid again and have my mother hold me and tell me that everything was going to be OK. I wanted her to take me home and help me find a way to change. I had finally hit my rock bottom.

23

After my suicide attempt, I attended some counselling sessions but they felt pretty much like box-ticking exercises. Though I pleaded with the counsellor to get me more time on the detox wing, it wasn't long before she declared me fit and I was back on a general wing again. This time, I was on Kingfisher.

I was still down but something had definitely changed. Whereas previously I had done crazy stuff to get through my time – attracting trouble with my hard-man act – now all I wanted was to get out as quickly as possible. That meant keeping my head down, even avoiding eye contact with any other prisoner who might want to start something with me. I was polite to the guards. I was a model prisoner.

After I'd served six months on remand, I went back to court for sentencing. Samuel wasn't representing me anymore but my new solicitor was optimistic. He submitted a psychiatrist's report detailing my suicide attempt and a letter I had written to the judge myself. Another inmate suggested it to me. The strategy hadn't actually worked for him but I figured I had nothing to lose. I poured my heart out onto the paper. I told the judge that I finally had a real desire to change and not ever go back to prison. I wrote about school and how I wished I'd taken more notice of the teachers who told me

I had potential. I wished I could have those opportunities again.

It worked. Based on the letter and the fact that I had already spent a fair bit of time locked up, I was released and Mum and Pete agreed to take me home.

Free from Feltham again, I went back to the house on the Richmond Road where Mum lived with Pete and my siblings, determined that this time things really would be different. Mum didn't need to tell me not to go in search of my old friends down by the river. I knew that if I had any chance of sticking to the decisions I'd made since I tried to kill myself, I had to stay away from anyone who might offer me drugs or even drink.

I'd promised Mum that I would go to a meeting with her – just to see what it was like – and a couple of days after I got home she decided it was time I made good on that promise. I agreed. As the moment got nearer, I could tell that Mum was excited. The meetings were really helping her and she was quietly determined that they would do the same for me.

Now that we had more time to talk, Mum told me how she'd come to realize she had to give up drinking. She said that one day she found herself on Richmond Bridge, looking over the edge, contemplating jumping off. It was a sunny Saturday. A really ordinary day. The bridge was busy with people heading for the town's shops and restaurants, and there Mum was, thinking about ending her own life. The only thing that stopped her was the fact that she had our family dog Pepe with her. She was in the middle of taking her for a walk.

When Mum got home that day, she called a recovery programme. That very evening, two female members came round to collect her and take her to her first meeting. She felt understood and cared for at last. Now she was evangelical about the twelve-step programme and didn't see any reason why it wouldn't work for everyone. She was certain it would work for me.

I could see that Mum was happy but I was sceptical. For a start, though I knew I had a problem with drugs, I was pretty sure I didn't have a problem with alcohol like Mum did. It was obvious that she was an alcoholic. Anyone who'd known her for any length of time would agree. I sometimes got so drunk I didn't know what I was doing, but when Mum was at her worst, she used to go and sit on a bench all day with the real alkies. The ones who got so drunk they forgot to wash or even undo their trousers before they took a piss. I'd never been that bad. Not with drink.

The meeting Mum wanted me to attend was on a Friday night. I wasn't impressed at the thought of spending a weekend night in a bare room at a London hospital, but a promise is a promise and I had already broken so many. I knew I was under a kind of probation at home. Of course, Pete was watching me closely to see if it was really safe for me to be back and around his kids.

'Just come along and see what you think,' Mum said. 'There's no pressure.'

I felt under enormous pressure but I agreed to go along anyway.

When we arrived at the hospital annex, a few people were already milling around outside smoking while they waited for the meeting to begin. They greeted Mum like an old friend. They were curious to know who I was and were warm and welcoming when Mum told them. They told me that Mum had spoken about me before and they were really pleased to have the chance to put a face to the name.

Everybody seemed nice enough but it struck me at once that they were all much closer to Mum's age than mine. I began to wonder if I was in the right place. I was a teenager. I'd got a bit out of control, that was all. What could I possibly have in common with these grown men and women whose ruddy cheeks were testament to years and years of drinking to excess? Decades. I wasn't going to head down that path.

Still, Mum wasn't going to let me slip away now. We went into the meeting room and took our places in the circle of plastic chairs. I asked Mum how the meeting would go. Would I have to say something? Would I have to stand up and say I was an alcoholic too?

'You don't have to say anything. Nobody has to do anything they don't want. But if you do feel like saying something, you can go for it. You might find it helps. Everyone will listen. No one judges anybody here.'

I looked at Mum. She sat on that hard plastic chair looking far more serene than she'd ever done in church. She was like a different woman. There was no doubt that she'd undergone some dramatic changes while I'd been inside. Was it really all down to this group, finally convincing her of the truth that no one had ever persuaded her to hear before?

I was envious of her calm. Though I insisted on keeping up the sceptical facade, I did want to know how she'd found it.

The group's members were all assembled now. Every chair was filled. I glanced around, trying to get the measure of the people who were there without staring too openly. My first impressions, based on the people we'd met outside, were not changed. I was the youngest by a long way. By a decade at least. There were two guys who looked as though they might be in their late twenties or early thirties, but everyone else was forty-plus. With their ravaged faces and broken bodies, they looked ancient to me. They might be sober now but it was obvious they'd been far further down the road to oblivion than I thought I ever had.

The man who took the chair introduced himself as Andy. He was maybe fifty. He said he had been sober for ten years. Looking at him, in his jumper and old-fashioned trousers, I decided at once there was nothing he could possibly say that would be relevant to me. I leaned back in my chair and crossed my arms. A closed-off position. Mum glanced at me. I could tell it made her anxious to see me look disinterested before the meeting had even properly begun. I uncrossed my arms and made an effort to at least look as if I was listening.

I didn't think Andy and I could have anything in common, but I was surprised to find that as he spoke there were a couple of things he said that rang a bell somewhere in my mind.

The two guys closest to me in age also spoke. One was called Bez. The other was Jamie. They were in their late twenties. Like me, Bez had been in prison. I sat up and listened a little more carefully when he told his story. He spoke about how hard it was to hang out with his old mates now that he was sober. He was realizing that all his friendships had revolved around drink and drugs. I understood that. Now that I was out again, I was itching to see my old mates. But how could I see them without joining in, getting drunk, getting stoned, getting back into all my bad habits?

Some of the old hands shared stories from their younger

171

days. The message seemed to be that Bez (and by extension me) would just have to get some new friends. Mum nodded in enthusiastic agreement. The thought of *never* being able to see my old mates again made me feel a bit ill. That seemed like a sacrifice too far.

By the end of the meeting, most of the people attending had said something. I didn't. By not speaking, I think I felt I could keep some part of myself back and hold everyone else at a distance. I'd decided that while it was an interesting enough experience and everyone had been very nice to me, it wasn't going to work. I couldn't see how it could. It was only talking.

'It ain't for me,' I said to Mum as we walked to the car.

She looked disappointed but she didn't push me on it. Not then, at least.

'If you change your mind,' she said.

Though I brushed off Mum's requests that I join her at another meeting, I was trying my hardest to start over in other ways. I needed to get some money and not by burglary or robbery. Pete got me a couple of jobs – helping his mates on building sites, that sort of thing. He even said I could work alongside him again on his burger van. There was nothing I wanted to do less, but I gave it my best for a little while. The money was shit and I hated going home smelling of cooking oil. Worst of all, I got bored and, the more bored I got, the more getting drunk and stoned appealed.

My old mentor Jake and his gang of mates had moved on. So had the kids who used to hang out with me and Ivan (who was still in prison). There was a new generation coming up in

Isleworth. I knew some of them. They were happy to have me around.

I was doing my best to stay away from seriously heavy drugs but soon I was smoking weed and drinking too much again. I didn't know how to turn them down. With no positive male role model to turn to at home, since my relationship with Pete was understandably even more difficult than before, and Mum absorbed in caring for my siblings and her own recovery, of course I went back to the only real fellowship I knew – that of the streets.

Mum was still going to meetings, but that winter she had a setback when she heard that her brother, my Uncle Tommy, had been killed.

The rumours had been swirling around for a while. A couple of years after that awful night in Belfast when Tommy tried to rekindle what he seemed to think of as some fucked-up mutual relationship with me (I later learned that abusers often try to convince themselves that their victims want them too) he was arrested for abusing two further children, one of them a girl.

It turned out that it wasn't the first time this girl had accused him of abuse either. The first time was five years earlier, but Tommy had threatened her that if she pressed charges there would be worse to come for her. Fearful of what might happen – Tommy still claimed he had IRA mates, after all – she let the charges drop.

It took a lot of courage for her to bring the charges a second time. Tommy was arrested at last. And two weeks later, he was dead.

The circumstances of Tommy's death were a mystery. He was found on the morning of 13 October 2001, unconscious and bleeding from a head wound. He was taken to the Royal Victoria Hospital but never regained consciousness and died five days later. He was thirty-three years old.

The attack had happened in an area of the city near the university that was popular with students looking for a cheap night out. It was a busy part of town, never quiet even in the early hours of a Sunday morning, so it seemed odd that no one came forward with any information about Tommy's movements that night. No one had seen anything. Nothing at all. Though he was found within spitting distance of some of the city's most popular pubs, not one person even spoke up to say they'd seen him in the hours before he died.

It's perhaps closer to the truth to say that no one *dared* say they'd seen anything. Or maybe no one particularly minded that he'd ended up with his head caved in. Tommy was a paedophile after all.

One of Tommy's drinking pals was eventually arrested over his death but he wasn't convicted. The evidence just wasn't there. And we all knew he didn't do it anyway.

I attended Tommy's funeral in Belfast with my mum. I don't know why. Perhaps I just wanted to make sure he was really gone. I even agreed to be a pall-bearer. As we walked into the tiny church that day, men well known to be members of the IRA flanked the path on both sides. They didn't come into the service, however. They weren't there to mourn Tommy Maughan or pay their respects. Nobody was going to miss that pervert. The IRA's presence that day was what's known as a 'show of strength'. Those men wanted us to know kiddy-fiddling was not acceptable on their patch. It's not unlikely that Tommy's murderer was among them. They were there as a warning that no paedo was safe while the IRA knew about it.

Though I was one of the four men who carried Tommy's coffin that day, 'rest in peace' were not the words on my lips either.

When, in 2014, I eventually told Mum what had really happened in Ireland, and all those years before in the Ivybridge flat, it broke her heart to find out that her little brother was a paedophile.

Mum managed to stay sober the whole time we were in Ireland for Tommy's funeral, but when we got back to London she fell off the wagon in a spectacular way, drinking to avoid the pain of what had happened to the little brother she loved so much. Drink was the fastest means of escape from reality we both had available to us.

However, Mum knew she had to cut her relapse short and was soon trying to get sober again. Meanwhile I was properly heading in the other direction. I was selling weed as well as smoking it now and using the proceeds to buy a bottle of brandy a day. My life was so shit, so boring and without any prospect of change that the only way to get through it was in a drunken haze.

The only good thing in my life, so far as I could see, was my new girlfriend, Hayley.

I met Hayley through the younger kids I'd been hanging around with since getting out of prison again. She was sixteen and had just finished school. She was beautiful. Just my type. She was fun too. She was always up for a party. And she liked me. She knew of my reputation of course, but that didn't put her off.

Like the girls who had written to me while I was inside, Hayley was attracted by my bad-boy persona. She liked my craziness. As soon as we got together, we were inseparable. I'd had plenty of girlfriends over the years but none came anywhere near what I felt for Hayley. This was different. We were in love.

So you would think I would want to be my best self for her. I suppose I did, but I didn't know how to go about it. I didn't know how to step back from the hard-man image and be a good man. I didn't know where to start. Instead I carried on selling weed, drinking and doing my best not to get a real job. And I was still a master of self-sabotage.

Shortly after we met, Hayley went on holiday to Turkey with her family. It was a trip she'd had planned since before we got together. It was only for a week. I was head over heels by this time and, though of course I didn't want to be apart from Hayley for even a day, I should have been able to get through it with the thought of how nice it would be to see her when she got back. Unfortunately, the moment we said good-bye and she set off for the airport, the doubts started creeping in.

At this point in my life, I'd never been anywhere except Isleworth and Ireland, and my imagination ran wild as I thought about Hayley's trip abroad. Turkey to me was crazily exotic, and Hayley was so gorgeous she would be surrounded by wealthy men living the kind of glamorous lives I could only dream about. With a load of rich blokes to choose from, why would she come back to me? As soon as she was away from me, her eyes would be opened to the fact that I was a loser. I had nothing. I'd been in prison. She deserved better. The chatter in my brain got louder and louder. Why would someone as good as Hayley want someone like me? And why should I trust her anyway? Everyone I'd loved so far had let me down eventually.

I got more and more angry and upset and so I convinced myself that while I was stuck in Isleworth, Hayley was cheating on me in some Turkish nightclub. The only way I could make myself feel better was to 'strike first' by being unfaithful myself. An old girlfriend – Jessica – had been in touch. While Hayley was away, I arranged to meet up with Jessica again. We got off our heads and went to bed.

I knew right away that I'd made a mistake. It hadn't changed the way I felt as I hoped it would. The next day, I told Jessica that I wasn't interested in getting back together with her. Hayley was the only one for me. Jessica seemed to be OK with that. A few days later, Hayley came home. She still wanted to see me. She told me she'd missed me like crazy. I didn't say anything about Jessica. I thought I'd got away with it.

But even with Hayley's love, I was still raising hell. Having pulled herself back from the downward spiral she got into after Uncle Tommy's murder, Mum was getting tired of my excuses for not trying to do the same. What's more, her relationship with Pete was under more strain than ever because of the way I was living.

Finally, Mum decided that she'd had enough. She told me that if I didn't sort myself out, I couldn't stay at home. I was causing too much disruption. Fortunately for me, Hayley and I were serious by then. She asked her parents if I could move in with them and amazingly they agreed that I could.

Hayley's stepdad, Steve, was a good man. He was physically intimidating. You wouldn't have wanted to get into a fight with him. But ultimately he was a big softy. He loved his family, valuing them above everything and doing all that he could to provide for them and give them a happy life. He drove articulated lorries and his hard-working ethic shone a light on everything I wasn't doing, but he didn't point it out to me in a heavy-handed way, which, given I was his stepdaughter's boyfriend, he would have been entitled to. He gently encouraged me to think about getting my act together through banter, which moved me to low-level guilt and shame in a way Mum and Pete's yelling had never done.

After I'd been living with the family for a while, Steve pushed me to get a job as a plasterer. It was hard work and I wasn't used to hard work but slowly I was beginning to understand that there's nothing quite like earning money instead of getting hold of it dishonestly. Unlike when Pete had asked me to work on his burger van to keep Mum happy and me out of trouble, I felt Steve was getting me work because he trusted me. That really boosted my self-esteem. With a proper wage packet in my hand, I booked my first foreign holiday. To Turkey. To the place where the successful people of my imagination went. I went with Hayley and had an amazing time. It motivated me in a way I hadn't imagined. It was a taste of what I could have if I worked hard enough.

Little did I know I was on the brink of losing it all again.

Almost a year had passed since I'd slept with Jessica while Hayley was in Turkey. I hadn't seen Jessica since that night. She hadn't been in contact. I assumed that, like me, she'd known that one night was a mistake and wanted it kept quiet. But she must have told someone because someone told Hayley.

Hayley didn't want to hear my excuses. She told me to get lost right away. And of course it wasn't just our relationship that was over. Hayley's family said I'd have to move out. Mum and Pete didn't want me back. Not only was I single. I was homeless.

I was desperate. I went back to couch-surfing, staying with whoever would have me for a night or two. It was only when I was away from them that I realized how well Hayley and her family had looked after me. I didn't know how to take care of myself. It got to the point where committing a crime and going back to prison started to seem like my only option. At least there I would be fed. I wouldn't have to worry about finding work.

In the middle of all this, I stayed a few nights with my friend Siobhan in Hampton. She decided to have a party. I was drinking, of course, and smoking. While the party happened around me, I sat there thinking of all the ways I'd fucked up. I didn't know how to pull myself out of the hole I was in. I didn't really want to go back to prison. After the last time, I didn't know if I could survive it. I felt like a cornered rat. All my escape routes were blocked.

Like a zombie, I got up from the sofa and went into the kitchen. I didn't talk to anyone on my way. There was no one else in there. I pulled the biggest knife out of the knife block and held it to my wrist. I think I just planned to give myself a little nick, to make myself feel better. But the knives were brand new and cut deeper than I expected. Before I knew what I'd done, blood was pouring from my wrist. I sank to the floor and slowly drifted into unconsciousness.

Thank God someone came into the kitchen for more drink. They called an ambulance. The crew patched me up but when they told me I needed to go to A & E for proper stitches, I refused to leave the house. By this time, the party was pretty much finished. No one wanted to stay after I'd put such a downer on the mood.

The ambulance crew gave up on me and left me with my friends. I just sat back down on the sofa and carried on drinking. Twelve hours later, Siobhan had had enough – she was scared that I was going to die on her – and somehow she got hold of my mum. By the time Mum turned up, my arm had swollen to twice its usual size. She insisted I went to the hospital.

At the hospital, the wound had to be drained before it could be stitched. I got the usual mental-health talk while I was being patched up but I said it was all a drunken accident so I wouldn't get sectioned. All the same, the gossip in my circle was that I'd finally lost it. My hard-man mask had slipped.

Soon, news of the incident got back to Hayley. Together with her mum, she came to visit me at Mum and Pete's. Pete had agreed to let me stay again to give the wound on my arm a chance to heal. Seeing me so pathetic made Hayley willing to listen to what I had to tell her about the Jessica incident at last. She accepted my explanation that I'd been listening to my inner demons. I'd behaved like a dickhead and an idiot because I didn't dare to trust that anyone would ever love me. I'd thrown everything we had away because I felt so worthless instead.

Hayley said she understood. She was willing to give me another chance. When I was well enough, I moved back in with Hayley and her family. They were endlessly patient and forgiving. Never judgemental. They made me want to be my best self. This time, I swore, I'd get it right.

I was doing my best to be a good boyfriend to Hayley. I'd ditched the heavy drugs. I'd ditched my loser friends. A year later, Hayley and I went on holiday to Crete where we met Kyle and Trisha, a couple from Belfast. We clicked straight away and spent the whole holiday hanging out with them.

I was spending time with people who had jobs and ambitions. I was making my own money and my own plans for the future. I had finally realized it was possible to live a normal life and enjoy it. Or at least it would have been, had I not made one more stupid mistake.

24

It was in July 2003 that I was arrested for the last time. It was for carrying an offensive weapon. In this case, a knife. It happened like this . . .

I'd gone out drinking in Hounslow with a few friends. We were all white lads, in a part of Hounslow which was predominantly not white. Towards the end of the night one of my friends got into a heated discussion with a Somalian man and his mates. They surrounded him, shouting and getting in his face. Getting wind of what was going on from across the pub, the rest of us headed over to calm things down. I apologized if my mate had caused any offence.

'He's drunk,' I said. 'He doesn't mean what he says.'

The Somalians seemed to be OK with that. But as we were walking away, the leader of their gang made a crack about us being 'pussy little white boys'. I turned round to face the guy and eyeballed him, though I knew there wasn't much I could do. They were mob-handed. So me and my mates just kept walking.

'Yeah, like the scared little bitch you are,' he said.

That last comment did me in. We left the pub and that should have been it but I couldn't let it go. The Somali guy's jibes had got to the very heart of me, where the little kid who got bullied at school still cowered deep inside. So many bad memories flooded back in an instant. The Somali guy got a direct hit on the scars left by Tommy's abuse, Pete's frustrated anger, Sid's rage, Pepsi's attempt on my life. My fragile self-esteem couldn't take it. The alcohol I'd been pouring down my neck all evening had robbed me of any capability of sensible judgement. It wasn't long before I'd decided I had to go back and show my latest tormentor who was boss.

Leaving my mates, I went home and found the six-inch blade I kept for exactly a moment like this. I made my way back to Hounslow alone. The Somali gang was still there. They were outside the pub, being loud and offensive to passers-by, grabbing girls who tried to get around them. I positioned myself at a bus stop nearby. With my baseball hat and hoodie I was invisible to them, as I'd intended. It was nearly closing time. All I had to do was wait.

When the pub closed, two of the gang went to the chicken shop for food. The rest walked towards the high street. The high street in Hounslow is pedestrianized. It's the perfect place for an ambush. No cars meant a lower chance of witnesses and an easier escape. I waited and watched from a distance until they reached the crossing onto the pedestrianized stretch, then I ran to catch up like a man possessed. I was powered by rage, fury and booze. I was going to stab that fucker in the neck. We'd see who the pussy was then.

Fate had other ideas. Just as I crossed the road, the traffic lights turned green and a police car pulled around the corner. The officer in the passenger seat looked straight at me. I had my hat on, my hoodie up and a knife in my hand. Our eyes met. I threw down the knife and kept running but it was already too late.

The police put their lights and sirens on and gave chase.

I was screwed.

I knew that, given my history, this relatively small offence (compared to the other stuff I'd done, at least) could be enough to send me back inside. So I took a risk. As Michael Maisey, I had a record as long as my arm, so I gave the arresting officer, who didn't know me or my backstory, my original birth name. Dad's name. I told him I was Michael Wright.

Michael Wright had a clean slate so when it came down to it, I got off lightly. Just a slapped wrist. A caution and home by bedtime. However, I knew that I'd been lucky and it probably wouldn't be long before the police made the connection between my two aliases. I decided that I needed to be long gone when that happened. I needed to do a 'geographic'.

A 'geographic' is a recovery term for when you try to solve a problem in your life by running away from it. By quite literally applying a geographical solution to the issue by physically moving somewhere completely different. The choice of where I would go came to me when me and Hayley saw our holiday friends Kyle and Trisha in December. They were living in Belfast. I asked them if I could stay in their spare room while I got myself established in Northern Ireland. They said they'd be happy to have me. I spent Christmas and New Year with Hayley and her family before moving to Ireland in January 2004.

It was a big deal for me and Hayley, my going to Ireland. We'd been together for almost three years by this point and we knew it was going to be hard to be apart. However, Hayley understood that if I stayed in London I would likely be back in prison before too long. I just couldn't seem to stay out of trouble when I was around my old mates and my old stomping grounds. It was better to have a long-distance relationship, where she could at least come and stay with me for weekends, than be back in prison, where she could only see me for an hour across a table under the watch of the guards.

Plus, I knew that going back to prison would kill me for real this time. I was still having nightmares about that last stay in Feltham and my suicide attempt. I would wake up in the middle of the night, remembering how it felt as the rope tightened around my neck or feeling the pain in my chest as the guards tried to resuscitate me. I couldn't go back there again. It would be the end of me.

So Belfast it was. Kyle and Trisha let me stay in their spare room and at first it was like being on holiday. Kyle and Trisha liked to party as much as me and Hayley did. Every night we'd be out, or if we stayed in we'd be drinking and smoking. Needless to say, I wasn't going to twelve-step meetings.

The trick that had saved me from another spell in prison worked in other contexts too. My birth certificate and NI number were both still in the name of Michael Wright, so I dropped the name Michael Maisey and all the shit that came with it when I was job hunting. It worked. The first job I got was as a security guard for Makro, a wholesaler in Dunmurry.

It was probably especially easy to get work on the night shift at Dunmurry because nobody in their right mind wanted it. The IRA had recently robbed the site I was hired to protect. As security guard, I was a sitting duck. I sat in a Portakabin on my own. That wasn't too bad. But what was freaky was when I had to make the rounds of the car park. I was an English kid with a skinhead. If the IRA came back, I wouldn't have looked like much of a threat. In fact, taking me out might have added to their fun.

I stuck out the security job for a couple of months but, even if I was crazy enough not to mind the constant threat of attack, I hated having to work nights when Kyle and Trisha were out partying without me. I needed something I could do during the day. So I applied for an admin position at the Northern Bank. My CV was pretty sketchy, but to my astonishment I aced the interview and got the job.

As I said, I wasn't going to twelve-step meetings in Belfast, though Mum kept hinting that I should. I had convinced myself that what I was doing was 'controlled drinking'. I was still of the opinion that so long as I wasn't actually swigging brandy out of a bottle in a brown paper bag on a park bench, I wasn't an alcoholic. I just liked to party, like any of my friends. We were only in our twenties. Getting drunk at the weekend was normal.

But in reality, my drinking was a problem and it was causing me to make bad decisions all the time. With the way I looked and the way I talked I already stuck out in Belfast in a bad way. Yet, when I'd had a few, I'd go drinking on the Falls Road, where Uncle Tommy used to take me. Remembering Tommy's IRA stories didn't put me off. I thought I could handle myself. I got into a lot of fights when just my being there pissed people off. I didn't give a fuck. I would fight anyone. And a lot of the time, I had my arse kicked. Being drunk didn't improve my boxing skills.

I was angrier than I had ever been. Belfast wasn't turning out like I'd hoped. I missed my friends. I missed my family. I missed Hayley, who was still in London with her mum and dad. Though we'd promised each other that it wouldn't, our relationship was suffering from being long distance.

Kyle and Trisha bought a bigger place. When they moved on, they rented their old flat to me. They were still good friends but we all needed some space. I left the Northern Bank for a job at a call centre. I was getting plenty of attention from girls. It was hard not to take advantage. One weekend, I talked to Hayley and said that I couldn't do long distance anymore. I was too young to be tied down by a girlfriend I didn't even get to see.

Hayley was devastated. She told me she missed me every day. She still loved me as much as she'd always done. A couple of days later, she called to tell me that she'd decided she was going to move to Ireland to be with me. She wasn't going to let me go. If I couldn't come back to London, she was coming to Belfast.

It seemed like the right decision. She turned up a couple of weeks later and moved into the flat I'd rented since moving out of Trisha and Kyle's. It was great to have her there. The fact that she'd given up everything – her job, her mates, being close to her family – to be with me meant a lot. No one had ever made that big an effort for me in my life before. I thought that having her around would help me to work out where I was going. Might help me start to get a handle on how much I was drinking.

I was still trying to stick to my 'controlled drinking' thing, but the fact was, once I'd had a couple of drinks, I didn't have an off switch. I was still hanging out in Catholic areas, shooting my mouth off and getting into fights. It's amazing that I hadn't been killed. I went to Catholic bars because my family were

Catholics, but my Englishness meant I didn't fit in. Likewise, I didn't fit in at the Protestant bars because I had been raised Catholic. I couldn't hold down a job. But given all Hayley had sacrificed to be with me, I knew I owed her my best effort at being a man worth moving countries for.

But I didn't want to go to any more meetings. No matter how bad I got, I still couldn't draw the parallel between me and the 'real' drunks. The drunks you crossed the street to avoid though you could still smell them from the other side. Drunks like my dead Uncle Tommy. That was what an alcoholic looked like. Alcoholics weren't young, like I was. They didn't look like I did. They didn't get up and go to work. They didn't have a girlfriend as beautiful and sexy as Hayley. A girlfriend who would give up so much to be with them.

I just needed a little bit of help breaking out of the cycle I was in. That was all.

It was Hayley who finally persuaded me to see a therapist. I was reluctant. Over the years since my first conviction, I'd seen plenty of shrinks and psychologists. I felt like I'd told my story a thousand times but no one had ever really heard it. The counselling sessions I'd had so far always felt like box-ticking exercises. Why should that change now? Still, I wanted to keep Hayley happy, so I went.

The therapist's name was David. He was youngish. Maybe in his thirties. We had two sessions, during which he began to draw out what was really going on with me. I spoke about the feelings I had around my family life growing up – the disappointment, the fear and the shame. Even the misplaced responsibility I felt for Dad leaving. David asked me questions that, remarkably, I'd never been asked before. He asked what were the steps that led to me drinking and what was the outcome of that first drink. I'd never put two and two together.

It was David who made me think that perhaps I did have a drink problem. I'd thought prior to talking to him that I was just fundamentally fucked. I picked fights because I was a psychopath. It was David who pointed out that I only really did crazy shit when I was drunk. And I got drunk because I was trying to numb my uncomfortable feelings. Therefore I needed to work on the feelings. Everything else would follow on from that.

After those first two sessions, David told me that he'd like to continue working with me, but because he knew I couldn't afford his rate he would drop it to ten pounds a time. He also suggested that I go to a meeting.

'Give it one more chance,' he said.

I said I'd think about it, though as I left his office I'd already made my mind up. Meetings weren't for me. I couldn't put a label on myself like the twelve-steppers did.

Later, I talked to Mum, who was still working hard to stay sober herself.

'It's a good idea, Michael,' she said. 'You only tried one. You should at least give it a second chance.'

So I told David that I would go to a meeting. He helped me to find one just two minutes from the flat I shared with Hayley. A meeting on my doorstep. It couldn't have been any easier. Was that a sign?

At my first Belfast meeting, I sat right at the back. I didn't talk to anybody. I felt just as out of place as I had at the meeting in the London hospital, though for different reasons. There,

I'd just been too young. Here, I was too young, too English and too hard-looking with my skinhead. I looked for all the ways I was different from the people who turned up. I was still fixated with finding all the reasons why they were alcoholics but I wasn't.

I wasn't an alcoholic because I wasn't old enough. I wasn't an alcoholic because I was holding down a job. I wasn't an alcoholic because I didn't smell of urine like one of the blokes who came into the meeting, more in hope of a free cuppa and a biscuit than help to cure his addiction, I thought. I ignored the fact that I'd frequently passed out through drinking and woken up in a wet bed.

The woman chairing the meeting was in her fifties and was deeply earnest. What did I have in common with her? We could not have been more different. Once again, just as in the hospital, I leaned back, crossed my arms and started to close down my mind.

The chair started to speak about her feelings around drinking, about how, even when she was drunk, she could be with her friends yet still feel alone. She could be in the middle of a room full of people yet she might as well have been standing in the middle of the desert. Life seemed to go on around her, not including her. She felt like she was always on the edges. I understood that feeling. Drinking was a way of feeling more confident, or feeling like it didn't matter. Then she spoke about how, no matter what she did, no matter how she succeeded on a day-to-day basis, she just couldn't feel good.

'No one understands,' she said.

I did. I recognized what she was saying.

I got home in a reflective frame of mind. Hayley was waiting for me.

'How did it go?' she asked anxiously. I knew it was important to her that something worked.

I shrugged.

'Will you go again?'

I still wasn't sure.

I still didn't think I needed to, but I agreed to keep going to therapy, at least.

25

I was coming up to my twenty-fifth birthday. I'd planned a trip back to London to celebrate. I thought that having been in Ireland for as long as I had, I could risk it. I wanted to see Mum and Maria and Sophie and Justin. Even Pete. I was looking forward to talking to Mum about the things I'd been working through in therapy. I was especially looking forward to seeing my kid brother and, Mum assured me, the same was true of him. Though I hadn't been much of a role model so far, for some reason thirteen-year-old Justin idolized me.

Mum was planning a whole weekend of family celebrations and I was determined to throw myself into everything. I was still slightly high on the good feeling I had from going to that Belfast meeting. I'd been sober for just a couple of weeks but I wanted Mum to be impressed with how much I'd changed. Everything was going to be different.

But deep down I was anxious about going back to London. I was anxious about seeing old faces and old rivals and what I would tell them when they asked me why I wasn't drinking anymore. Then when I landed at Heathrow, I got a phone call that changed the course of the weekend. It was one of my old mates.

'Maisey! I hear you're back in town! A load of us are meeting at the pub tonight. Come and join us.'

'I can't,' I said. 'My mum's got loads of stuff planned. I can't go down the pub.'

'Don't say that, Maisey. You can come and have one drink with us first.'

Yes, I decided. Yes, I could. Just one drink would be fine. I hadn't seen my mates in a long while. It would be good to catch up. I would have one drink and still be back home in time for dinner.

So, I dropped my stuff off at Mum's and, batting away her pleas that I should be careful, I went to the pub. Of course I would be careful. I promised I would be back at Mum's by the time Justin and Sophie got home from school.

I was not home by the time Justin and Sophie got home from school.

I stayed in the pub all afternoon as more and more of my old mates turned up. I didn't need to buy a drink that day. It was like the first time I got out of Feltham. Everyone was delighted to see me. Everyone wanted to get me a pint or a shot. I accepted every one. I was soon completely smashed. Someone gave me a wrap of coke. I went into the gents' and snorted the first of several lines. Having stayed away from coke for quite a while, I was amazed at how quickly it hit me. I was tired from having travelled over from Belfast but the coke lifted me up. A couple more lines and I was ready to stay out all night.

When last orders were called and the pub closed, we went to a party, where more of my old friends were waiting. I danced and drank and did more lines. Someone had some crack. I had to share some of that. The floodgates were open. I juggled drugs to keep me awake and buzzing yet mellow throughout the wee small hours. I didn't tell Mum where I was. Hayley's calls went unanswered. Alcohol and drugs had opened the doors of my cage. I was free.

The next day, I was in the pub again as soon as it opened. This time I was buying the drinks and there were loads of them to buy. I missed the family barbeque Mum had planned for that afternoon. Calls from her and from Hayley continued to stack up on my phone. From time to time, I checked my phone and saw they'd tried to find me. It made me feel hunted so I ignored the messages and had another drink to dilute my annoyance that Hayley and Mum were trying to spoil my fun.

Day turned into night. My mates and I went clubbing, then to another party. I fell asleep on the sofa in a random house. I didn't even know who lived there. My clothes were getting dirty. I didn't care, so long as someone nearby had a can or a spliff I could have.

I couldn't remember when I'd last had such a good time. When I'd last felt like life was fun. Since Hayley got me to go to the therapist, she was determined that I stuck to what he advised. Hayley and I weren't having fun anymore. I was glad she'd decided not to come to London with me. That weekend was a break from reality.

And I was totally detached from reality. I had spent the past forty-eight hours inebriated. I never had an empty hand. I was always holding a bottle or a joint, trying to hang on to the feeling that life was easy, good and free. Why didn't Hayley understand that? Or Mum? Why did they want to tie me down and clip my wings?

My party companions understood. They knew how hard I worked. I had the right to a good time. It was nearly my birthday.

I didn't get back to Mum's until the following day – Sunday – and then it was only because I needed to pick up my stuff before the flight back to Belfast.

When Mum opened the door, she just shook her head. I swept in, thinking that I could make up for the weekend's absence with a few precious minutes, but my brother could barely look at me. He sat on the sofa, staring at his trainers. He had waited weeks to see me. Over the phone I'd told him I couldn't wait to see him too. But I had not spent any time with him that weekend at all. I'd missed everything Mum had planned. Everything Justin had been looking forward to. The disappointed look on his face cracked my heart in two.

'How could you do it?' Mum asked. 'Your brother has been waiting all weekend to see you. Doesn't he matter to you anymore?'

'Of course, Mum, but—'

She didn't want to hear my excuses. She waved them away and said, 'Son, you need to look at your drinking.'

I wanted to disagree but I couldn't. She was right. Was this the proof I needed at last? Proof I was an alcoholic?

Mum hugged me briefly then sent me on my way.

'You're going to miss your plane.'

The flight home was no fun. I felt every bit of the hangover I deserved as the plane came to a bumpy landing. Worse was to come. When I got back to Belfast, I still had to face Hayley. She already knew that things hadn't gone well. I couldn't pretend that I hadn't answered her calls all weekend because I lost my phone or something like that because of course, in her worry, she'd called Mum. What Hayley didn't yet know was that I had spent everything we had in our joint account on alcohol and drugs and payday was still a very long way off.

She had every right to be furious.

'You're pathetic,' was all Hayley said as she went to bed without me.

That weekend was a serious low point. Another rock bottom. I loved my little brother so much. Seeing the disappointment on his face when I swung by the house to pick up my luggage was more effective than looking in a mirror the morning after the night before.

I vowed to make an effort again. I promised Hayley that this time, this time, she could trust me. I never wanted to upset her or Mum or Justin like that again. I needed to go back to David and get his help to work out what triggered me to go on benders such as I'd just had. It couldn't just be that I was a selfish bastard, I hoped.

On my actual birthday, instead of going out, I went to a recovery-group meeting. I listened to several other people talk before I had the courage to speak up and tell the tale of my lost weekend. I understood why Mum and Hayley had been so angry with me but it was a relief to be around people who weren't going to judge me. When I said that I wanted to take control of my drinking, they believed me.

26

For the next three months, it seemed to be working. I went to three or four meetings a week. I didn't go out. I just went to the meetings and listened to the stories then I went straight home. I was still the youngest at the meetings by a long way but I was beginning to understand that what made an alcoholic had nothing to do with how someone looked, how old they were or what church they claimed to belong to. It was about what alcohol does to you emotionally. I was learning that I was the same as that fifty-something woman in the chair, the same as Andy, Jamie and Bez back in London. I was the same as Mum. I drank because I was trying to escape myself.

It worked. For the next few months, I did not touch a drop of alcohol. I did my best to avoid the people and places I associated with getting drunk or stoned. I carried on my sessions with David. I went to as many meetings as I could. I listened to the stories of dozens of other alcoholics. I was convinced that I was doing everything I could. I was nailing it. I could get sober no problem. I wasn't a thoroughbred drinker. I was a binge drinker. I drank when I was anxious – such as when Mum organized that massive weekend for me. I drank when I was angry. I was starting to know my triggers. I didn't need to get a sponsor and work the twelve steps. I just needed to keep up the meetings for a few months then I would be fine. Cured.

No one was a bigger support to me during those months than Hayley. Despite my having let her down so badly, she was always ready to listen or offer me a cuddle. Her whole family had been so good to me. Even after they heard what happened when I went back to Isleworth for the weekend, they were willing to give me another chance. Hayley's stepdad Steve was one of the few men in my life who'd seen potential in me. He liked me so much that when he and Hayley's mum Caroline decided to get married, he asked me to be his best man.

The wedding date was set for the end of September. They'd chosen an all-inclusive resort in Jamaica as the venue. Hayley was over the moon at the idea of a holiday in the Caribbean. I was too. All through July and August, while I sat in those meetings and told myself I was working hard on getting sober, that trip to Jamaica seemed like the perfect reward, encouraging me to keep going.

However, when I told some of the people at the meeting that I was going away they weren't so keen on the idea. An all-inclusive resort? Free drink on tap? I was putting myself in harm's way.

'Don't go,' one of them told me bluntly. 'Don't put yourself in a situation where everyone else will be drinking, Michael. You'll never resist it.'

But how could I not go? The trip had been booked for months. I was going to be Steve's best man. If I didn't go, Hayley would be gutted. Steve and Caroline would be disappointed. He'd lose the money he'd already spent on my flight.

Plus, I wanted to be on that beach. I needed a break. I needed sunshine. A free holiday in the Caribbean? Nothing was going to stop me.

I was convinced that it would be fine. I packed a copy of the 'Big Book' with my sunglasses and swimming trunks. It was the book that all the people who went to meetings clutched like a bible. It wasn't exactly a beach read, but I was sure it would protect me from all the temptations I was likely to encounter. Every time I felt like having a drink, I would reach for the Big Book instead. It'd be like having a meeting in my suitcase.

My friends at the meeting wished me luck. I didn't think I'd need it.

We flew to Jamaica. I'd never seen anywhere so lovely. Leaving rainy Belfast and touching down in the Caribbean was like going to heaven. I couldn't think of anything better than the days that stretched ahead. Two weeks in the sun with a bunch of people I loved being around. To think that I might have turned it down? Crazy.

Steve and Caroline had booked us into a seriously amazing resort. It was like paradise. Our rooms overlooked the sea and a beach with sand as white and fine as sugar. The food was amazing and there was as much of it as you could eat. The drinks were free. Still, I managed to turn them down, and, knowing what I had been going through the past few months, no one in the party tried to push one on me. When I asked for a Coke instead of a beer, Hayley squeezed my hand and told me she was proud of me. With the sun, the sea and the company of Hayley, I was sure that getting through the trip without a sniff of alcohol was going to be a breeze, even though it soon became clear that alcohol was a big part of the all-inclusive thing.

Back in Belfast, I hadn't set foot in a pub since my birthday-weekend bender. At the resort, I couldn't avoid it. Most of the socializing happened at the pool bar. It was an unusual experience, watching people getting drunk when I wasn't drinking myself. I got a glimpse into how quickly alcohol can make people change. How loud and obnoxious they can get after a few drinks too many. How boring.

I just kept drinking Coke and going back to our room to read the Big Book when it all got too much for me. In the mornings, I felt happy and even slightly smug when I was the first of our party on the beach because I didn't have a hangover. That felt really good.

But by day four, I was starting to feel a little differently. Though they knew that I wasn't supposed to be drinking and didn't try to make me change my mind, Hayley and her family didn't let my being sober keep them from having a good time. After a while, the smug feeling I got from being sober while they were all smashed started to wear off and instead I decided that I was feeling bored. I also felt increasingly isolated. I just couldn't join in with the conversations in the same way. I found the jokes that had everyone else rolling around really stupid. But I wanted to join in the conversation and I wanted to get the jokes. I felt left out.

So, on the fourth day of the holiday, I sat Hayley down and told her that I couldn't stay stone-cold sober while everyone else started drinking straight after breakfast. Obviously, there was no way I could ask Hayley and her family not to go to the bar, so I came up with another plan. I was going to try controlled drinking again.

'I'll just have a couple to take the edge off,' I said.

Hayley shook her head. 'You can't,' she said. 'You know what will happen if you do.'

'Nothing will happen,' I insisted. 'I'm just going to have a couple of beers. I'm not going to get drunk. You can keep an eye on me and tell me when I've had enough.'

'You never listen to me when I tell you you've had enough,' she pointed out.

'Maybe I never used to, but I'm different now, Hayley. I know I've got a problem and I need to be careful. It's just that I'm finding it really hard. I feel left out because I'm not drinking. I feel like everyone's having a really great time and I'm not.'

The sun, the sand and the sea were not enough.

Hayley didn't want to agree with me but she could see that I'd already made my mind up. The next time we were in the bar – that evening after dinner – I ordered my first proper drink of the holiday. Just a light beer. A small one. The barman placed the bottle in front of me with a smile. The bottle was so cold that condensation soon started forming on the glass to match the sweat on my forehead as I thought, just for a second or two, about what I was about to do.

I'd not touched alcohol in months. I had been doing really well. I knew I felt better when I wasn't drinking. It wasn't just that my skin and my eyes were clearer without booze. My mind was clearer too. Much clearer. Did I want to risk that clarity?

The bottle sat in front of me on the bar. Though the sun was going down it was still thirty degrees outside. I knew how good it would feel to take a nice long swig of that ice-cold liquid.

Come on, said the voice in my head. *It's OK. It's not going to kill you. You deserve it. You've gone nearly three months without anything. You'll just have a couple and then lay off it again. It will be easy.*

I raised the bottle to my lips. Oh my God. It was like the best kiss I could ever remember. The beer slid down my throat like liquid gold. I tried to make it last, reminding myself with every sip that I was only going to have two and they had to last me the rest of the evening, but the first bottle was soon gone. The barman already had another one lined up.

I was right about one thing, having a couple of beers did make me feel better. Almost right away, my mood changed. I didn't feel like I was sticking out anymore. I felt more relaxed around Hayley's family and I was sure they felt more relaxed around me as well. I was aware that drinking in the company of somebody who can't could feel awkward. If any of the gang were concerned that I'd broken my three-month spell of sobriety to have those beers, then they didn't say anything. Instead, they reached out their own bottles to chink against mine in toast after toast. Everybody was having a really good time. The setting sun, the mellow music, that melting feeling of getting slowly sloshed . . .

Hayley said something to me part way through the evening. 'You've had way more than two. You said you wouldn't. I think you ought to stop now.'

I brushed her complaint away.

'I'm having a good time,' I said. 'And I'm in control. If it's starting to bother you, you can always go and sit somewhere else.'

The aggression in the way I responded to her concern was a sure sign that I wasn't in control and Hayley knew it. But what could she do? She didn't want to spoil the holiday atmosphere with an argument. Instead, she went for a walk around the resort, while I stayed with her cousins.

Hayley's cousins were going up and down to the bar like a pair of ants bringing food back to the nest. Every time they got themselves a drink, they got one for me too. After all, everything was included. None of us had to pay for the rounds we were getting in. I was soon drinking two drinks to every one Hayley's cousins put away. A switch had flipped in my brain and I was no longer counting.

The evening slipped away. I had a couple more beers and then I suggested a night cap. Or three. Hayley's cousins were only too pleased to join me. I mixed beers with rum punch and other cocktails that tasted like kids' drinks but had a lethal kick.

Hayley eventually gave up on persuading me to slow it down and went to bed. I promised I would join her later. I was just going to listen to some more of the reggae that I'd grown to love while sharing a cell with Dredd back in my Feltham days. However, when the bars closed at one in the morning, I was still ready to party on. I felt good. I felt like myself again.

The resort gave the impression that Jamaica was an idyll where nobody had to worry about anything except finding a shady spot to sleep off a hangover, but the truth of the island outside the manicured gardens was very different from the glossy-travel-brochure-worthy views. The gates to the resort weren't just guarded, they were guarded by armed men with assault rifles and pistols. We'd even been warned as we checked in that if we left the resort and ventured out into the town beyond, it was absolutely at our own risk.

The guards reiterated that warning as, together with Hayley's cousins, I left the resort, with its closed bars, to go in search of an off-licence.

We laughed at their warnings. How rough could paradise be? Besides, alcohol still had the same effect on me as it did back when I drank a bottle of Thunderbird to face the school bullies. It fired me up. With alcohol inside me, I could face down anyone.

That night, we found an off-licence and came back loaded down with the local beer and rum. See, we said to the guards as they let us back in through the gates. Nothing to be scared of. We took the booze up to the cousins' room and drank it on their balcony, keeping the neighbours awake.

I got to bed in the small hours – pissing Hayley off as I clambered in beside her – and woke up with the kind of hangover that can only be cured by the hair of the dog. After breakfast, I found myself in the bar again, while the grinning barman who'd served me my first beer the day before lined up two more to save me making another trip.

I was up and down to the bar all day and, once more, when the bar closed, I still wasn't ready to finish drinking. It was time to risk the outside world again. Once again the guards warned us that they had no responsibility for us as soon as we were past the gates. I laughed. I'd done it before. I knew there was nothing to worry about.

This time, Hayley's brother Perry and two Irish blokes we'd met in the pool bar came with me to the off-licence. It might have been OK but one of the Irish blokes was a mouthy drunk, and while we were on our way to the offy he got into an altercation with a local. Walking ahead with Perry, I didn't hear the remark that kicked everything off, but it got nasty pretty quickly. However, we were four and the Jamaican guy was on his own. He was a big guy but faced with the prospect of four-on-one, he soon backed off. We thought that would be the end of it.

So we went into the shop and stocked up on beer and rum. When we got what we needed, Perry and I walked out ahead of the Irish guys. We had no trouble. But when the Irish guys came out of the shop, they were mobbed. The local they'd insulted was back and this time he had his mates with him. Like goldfish that had fallen into a tank of piranhas, the Irish guys were stripped of everything they had in a matter of seconds. And then the locals turned their sights on Perry and me.

We legged it but by this time it was twenty-on-two and we weren't the ones who had the numerical advantage. Doing my best to hang on to the alcohol, I battled with at least five guys at once. Meanwhile, Perry launched a bottle of Coke at the locals coming up behind. It caught one of them square in the face. We were in deep trouble now. Abandoning the beers, we ran for our lives. Thank God the security guys saw us coming. They got ready to let us in and keep our pursuers out. The bottle of Coke Perry lobbed had only made things worse. We didn't have anything else to throw. The hotel security guards gave us cover – firing threatening shots into the air – until we were safely behind the gate. No one was hurt, but the guards left us in no doubt that they were ready to shoot to kill if they had to. Did we get why it wasn't safe to leave the resort now?

*

The following morning at breakfast, news of our narrow escape was on everyone's lips. Everybody knew about it. Half the guests regarded me and Perry with awe. The other half looked at us in horror. We'd brought reality crashing into their holiday. They couldn't pretend that Jamaica was such an idyll anymore.

I promised Hayley that I had left the resort for the last time. It had come way too close to getting really nasty.

'You know you wouldn't even have taken the risk if you weren't drinking,' she said.

I agreed. 'I swear I won't do it again.'

But Hayley was finding out that promises made with a hangover are worth about as much as promises made while drunk. The Big Book lay unread in the hotel room while I carried on partying. For a third day in a row I started drinking after breakfast and carried on all day. I drank until all the hotel bars closed. Then, for a third day in a row, I left the hotel compound – alone this time – and headed for the off-licence.

'You're crazy,' the guards told me. 'You're going to get yourself killed.'

I didn't care. I was on a mission.

All those months when I hadn't been drinking, I'd found it easy to stay away from drugs too. If I didn't drink, I didn't feel anything like the same need to use. But I'd broken my sober streak and the alcohol had reopened the gaping need for oblivion at the heart of me. The cravings I had fought to suppress were back with a vengeance. I wanted to change the way I felt and drugs were the fastest way.

It was easy enough to find someone to oblige me. Stupid drunk, I got into a car with a huge Rastafarian guy and let him drive me deeper and deeper into the ghetto. It was an idiotic move. I was an English guy with a skinhead and an England football shirt. I had a wallet full of cash. I might as well have had 'sucker' tattooed on my forehead. Of course I knew I was probably making a huge mistake, but the hunger for drugs was stronger than any sense of self-preservation right then. I decided to put on my game face, just like I used to in Feltham. If I looked enough of a nutter, I'd be OK.

We pulled up outside a shack made of corrugated iron. There the Rasta introduced me to one of his friends who said he could get me anything I desired. What I wanted right then was cocaine. He had it.

I bought enough coke to keep me going for the rest of the holiday but I was so keen to get it into my system that I asked the dealer if I could take some in his house before I set off again. Of course I could. The dealer brought me a can of Red Stripe while I chopped out a couple of lines on a battered table.

It was the first time I'd snorted coke since the weekend before my birthday when I let my mum and brother down so badly – but I didn't let that memory put me off. As the drugs worked their way into my bloodstream, I felt invincible again. I got loud. I was full of confidence. Every sensation was heightened. I didn't give a shit about where I was and the sort of danger I might be in anymore. I simply felt good. As the cocaine flooded my system, I was as happy in the dealer's filthy house as I had been at the pristine resort.

I just wanted to stay there forever, talking shit and feeling like nothing in the world could touch me and hurt me again. Could I stay? My new friend smiled and nodded. I could hang out as long as I wanted. He handed me another can of Red Stripe. I loved Jamaica.

I snorted everything I had bought to last me for the rest of the trip that first night. People came and went. They shared their drugs with the dealer and with me. I smoked ganja stronger than anything I'd ever had at home. I handed over the rest of my money for as much coke as it would buy.

Hours passed and soon daylight began to creep through the broken shutters of the dealer's house. Outside, the sun warmed the golden sand. Birds sang to greet the new day. The traffic started up. Reggae music blared from a passing van. Holiday-makers were heading for the beach. Outside was Jamaica in all its colourful glory. I stayed in the gloom of the dealer's house and offered him my watch in return for another wrap.

I was missing for nearly two days. After what had happened the night before I disappeared, with the twenty-strong gang chasing me and Perry back into the resort, everyone assumed that I'd fallen foul of the same people. I'd gone out on my own and they'd got me. Hayley and her family organized a search party to look for me. The resort staff did their best to help but they didn't hold out much hope. There was every chance I was already dead.

I was oblivious to what was going on back at the hotel. I didn't worry. I simply didn't think about it. Time meant nothing to me while I was high and I was higher than I had ever been. The dealer kept it coming. Beer, weed, coke. I had no reason to move.

But eventually I ran out of money and my new friend ran out of hospitality.

'Time for you to go,' he said.

I stepped out into the sunlight, shielding my sore red eyes. I had no idea how much time had passed. I didn't even know where I was.

I had no money for a taxi. I had no phone to call anyone to get them to come and find me. But on the horizon I thought I could see the beach. I told myself that if I could get to the beach, all I had to do was keep walking and eventually I would find the hotel. Getting to the sand, I walked in the blistering heat for what felt like hours until in the distance I noticed a group of people waving their hands in the air. I thought it was odd. I didn't think for a moment it had anything to do with me. But then someone shouted, 'We found him!', and I realized I had stumbled into my own search party.

When I finally got back to the resort, Hayley's joy at my return was short-lived. Once she'd established that I wasn't hurt and I hadn't actually been kidnapped and held against my will, she was furious. The wedding was taking place that afternoon. While I'd been snorting coke with a bunch of Yardies, Hayley and her family had been wondering whether they should call the wedding off and start a murder inquiry instead.

I apologized but Hayley was furious.

Now I was back, the wedding would go ahead. But was I in any fit state to be best man?

'You've got to talk to Dad,' Hayley said.

I could think of nothing I wanted to do less.

I was sweating, nasty alcoholic sweat, as I walked down the corridor to Steve's room. Hayley walked ahead of me. I could tell by the set of her shoulders that I wasn't forgiven. With every step closer to Hayley's stepdad, I felt worse. I could only imagine how angry he was going to be.

When he saw me, he shook his head.

'Look at the state of you. Where the fuck have you been?'

My head pounded and I wanted to throw up, but I knew I was going to get no sympathy from Steve. I had almost ruined the wedding. Might still ruin it.

'I'm sorry, Steve,' I said. 'I don't know what happened. Well, I do. I shouldn't have had a drink. I think the pressure of being out here for the wedding was getting on top of me. I thought a couple of drinks would help, but I can't have a couple of drinks. And then I met this Yardie . . .'

I told the whole story.

Basically, I had a breakdown in front of Hayley's family. They accepted my apologies. I don't think they wanted to do anything else right then. They had a wedding to get ready for. I assured Steve that I would still be able to get through the best-man duties without making a fool of myself.

'Good,' he said. 'Because it's all going to be on film.'

I'd forgotten that he'd hired a professional videographer to capture the whole day for posterity.

'Just don't have anything else to drink before the ceremony,' Steve said.

I went back to the room I was sharing with Hayley to get dressed for the ceremony ahead. Though the room was air-conditioned, I couldn't stop sweating. I felt worse than I had in a long time. The drink and drugs combined had completely fucked up my ability to keep my body temperature down. I tried showering but that didn't help for long, and I was going to have to put on a shirt and tie for the wedding. What I needed was the hair of the dog. Only I knew there was no point asking Hayley to get me something to drink. She was getting ready herself. She had barely said a word to me for hours.

That's when I spotted two half-pint glasses on the table on

our balcony. They'd been there since I left them there, two nights before. They were each half-full but what remained was hardly appetizing. Couldn't have been further from the ice-cold beer that broke my three-month spell of sobriety. These leftover beers were as warm as blood and floating with flies and God knows what else. No one in their right mind would have wanted to drink them. But I wasn't in my right mind. To me, they suddenly looked like the solution.

I scooped out the flies with my fingers then, wincing, I knocked back those dregs like I was a man finding water in the desert after a week-long crawl across the sand. The taste made me want to vomit but I knew that, if I could just keep it down for a minute or two, it would start to work its magic. It worked. That fag-end-flavoured beer was just enough to let me get to the wedding gazebo on the beach, get through the ceremony and deliver the world's shortest and possibly worst best man's speech.

After that, I drank a few more times – I had to toast the bride and groom, right? – but I didn't go off the resort again. I did, however, manage to get into a fight with some American guests, who disapproved of the way I was behaving when I was drunk. It started out verbal, then I threw a few punches that didn't land. All in all, I made a proper fool of myself. It's a wonder that Hayley and her family didn't opt to leave me behind when we all flew home.

On the flight back, I was covered in shame. I wanted to wind the clock back to that moment when the barman put the first beer in front of me and tell him, 'No thanks.' But I hadn't.

That plane journey was a reflective one to say the least. It was a night flight. Around me, everyone was sleeping but I was still buzzing from all the cocaine I had taken days earlier. I couldn't concentrate on the little screen on the back of the seat in front of me. All I could do was replay the events that had led to me finding myself in this place again. Making the same mistakes again. Upsetting the people I loved.

I had let everybody down. Hayley. Steve and Caroline. Especially myself. I needed to change. I had to. I promised Hayley that I would go to a meeting as soon as we got back but I was dreading it. I thought I knew what they would say.

27

Thankfully, my friends at the twelve-step meeting in Belfast, who had advised me not to go to Jamaica at all, were not judgemental when I told them how the trip had panned out. No one said 'I told you so' – even though they had told me so – because all of them had experienced the same thing in one way or another. They all knew what it was like. Being sober for a little while, thinking you had it nailed, thinking you could get away with having a couple of drinks only to find it led to going off the rails in spectacular fashion.

Back home in Belfast, doing my best not to drink again, I felt ill when I thought about the risks I'd taken in Jamaica when I was drunk. I'd followed a Yardie coke dealer into a ghetto. It could have all ended so differently. I was lucky to get out with my life.

Hayley was still determined to help me sort my life out. I don't know what it was she saw in me but she was willing to put everything that had happened behind her and try again. She was a truly lovely woman. Beautiful and kind. She could have chosen from any number of men but she chose me. The man who nearly ruined her family wedding. The man who plumped for drinking over spending time with his younger brother. The man who had spent a month's worth of rent and grocery money in a single weekend on the lash. I was the furthest thing from Prince Charming. But Hayley still loved me and she continued to think that if she loved me just a little bit harder I would start to change for the better.

Seeing Hayley's blind trust in me did make me want to try harder.

I went back to the meetings. The first one was the very day we got back from Jamaica. After that I got into a routine of doing three or four a week again, listening to my fellow addicts and trying, really trying, to learn something from their lives.

At the same time, I got a new job. When I wasn't drinking, I was good at dealing with people. I knew how to turn on the charm. As Michael Wright, I got a customer service position at Fleet Financial, a car-hire firm that looked after fleets of vehicles for big corporations. It was a nice job with potential to move up through the ranks. The boss of the privately owned company was a self-made man and he seemed to like me. He had no idea about the emotional baggage I was carrying. He certainly didn't know I'd been inside. He seemed to think that, with a bit of investment on his part, I could become a real asset to the firm. I promised him I would live up to his expectations.

I did my best but not all the people in the office were as keen on me as the big boss was. Perhaps it was precisely because the big boss liked me that they didn't. There were a couple of women in particular who seemed to have a problem with me. Whenever I walked into a room they would suddenly stop talking, giving me the impression that they must have been talking about me. If they spoke to me at all, it was with disdain.

I tried to ignore it. I didn't say anything. After Jamaica, I was on a sort of probation, at home and in my head. I wanted to prove to myself that I could live a normal life. I didn't have to get drunk or high and I didn't have to involve myself in the kind of office politics that would only make me angry. I just kept my head down around my colleagues and concentrated on hitting my targets. At home, I did my best to reassure Hayley that I was working hard on being a better boyfriend.

Christmas soon came around. Of course, I was invited to the office Christmas party. By coincidence, it was taking place the same night as Hayley's work do. I was disappointed that meant Hayley wouldn't be coming with me to mine. I'd been counting on her moral support. Had she come with me to my party, or had I gone to her party instead, things might have turned out very differently.

I must have had a sense that the office party could go badly. The night before, I went to a twelve-step meeting. There was a man there, Sean, who I'd recently started to confide in. He had been sober for the best part of thirty years. He had something about him. There was an air of freedom in the way he carried himself and the way he talked. I envied him that. I looked up to him as the kind of uncle I wished I'd had. The kind Tommy had never been. I told him that the party was coming up and that I didn't think I could get through it without having a drink. Sean said he understood. He'd been there many, many times. Then I floated the idea by him that I could have a couple of drinks without doing too much damage. Sean just smiled and shook his head.

'This is Jamaica all over again, Michael. Don't go to the

party if you think you're going to be tempted. You know there's no such thing as controlled drinking. Just don't go. Come to a meeting instead.'

I respected Sean and I understood what he was trying to tell me but the voice in my head was far louder than his right then. And the voice in my head was telling me that I couldn't stay home. No way. Everyone from the office would be at that party. If I stayed home, people would want to know why. Nobody at the office knew about my problem with drink so I couldn't tell them that was the reason. They'd gossip behind my back. I was already feeling paranoid about the way some of my colleagues treated me. I didn't want to give them any more ammunition. I had to go and I had to have at least a couple of beers to put them off the scent.

I told Sean I would think about what he'd said but the fact was, as I left the meeting, I already knew I was going to that party. And I knew I was going to drink. And I also knew, at least on some level, that the only possible outcome was chaos.

Dressed for her own Christmas party, Hayley looked stunning. I couldn't help but be jealous of the people who would get to spend time with her that evening. Were there any men among them who might try it on?

'Don't be stupid,' Hayley told me. 'I'm all yours.' She hugged me tight. I told her I believed her.

Before we went our separate ways we talked about the evening ahead. Hayley echoed Sean's advice, telling me that I didn't have to go to my party at all if I thought it might go badly.

'No one will care. After they've had a couple of drinks, they won't even know whether you're there or not.'

I didn't think that was true. I thought my absence would make everyone think I was stuck-up.

'OK. Then just don't drink,' she said. 'No one will notice, I promise, once they've all had a few. They won't care that you're not drinking. You've been doing really well, Michael. Please just have a Coke or something. Think how good you'll feel tomorrow morning, waking up without a hangover while everyone else feels like shit.'

'Maybe you shouldn't drink either?' I suggested.

'I'll only have a couple,' Hayley said.

I didn't push it. I knew that I couldn't ask her not to drink just because I had a problem with it. Her taxi had arrived. We kissed goodbye.

The Fleet Financial party was being held in a fancy hotel on the coast. Everyone had made a real effort. I hardly recognized some of the people from the office in their fancy party clothes. The boss was waiting by the door to greet us all. He shook my hand as I walked in.

'Glad to have you with us, Michael,' he said. We chatted a bit about how I'd enjoyed my first few months at the firm. The boss knew I'd hit all my targets.

'You could go a long way,' he told me.

It was good to hear and I would have liked to talk more but another newcomer had arrived so I joined my colleagues by the bar. Someone asked me what I wanted. The bar was free. I told them I would have a beer.

None of my colleagues knew I was in recovery so none of

them questioned my request. I got my beer. It was like a comfort blanket. As soon as I had it in my hand I felt like I could get through the night ahead. That first drink I nursed for as long as I could, still telling myself that I was going to stick to two, max. But by the time I was halfway down the second pint, I was loosening up on my criteria. By the time I'd had three, I'd forgotten all my promises to Hayley and myself.

Our boss had really pushed the boat out that night. As well as the drink, there was free food. If I'd had more of that food, maybe it would have slowed my drinking down, just a little. I stayed by the bar. The beers kept coming. I felt the old Michael taking over. I was louder, funnier and happier than the Michael my colleagues knew.

I was having a much better time than I expected, but after a while I couldn't shake the feeling that the women who seemed to have a problem with me in the office were building up to something again. Every time I glanced in their direction it seemed like they were looking at me. It wasn't just once or twice. It happened five or six times. They'd be staring at me then quickly look away and lean in close to each other. I was sure they were talking about me. Why else would they look so shifty when I caught their eye? Worrying what they were saying made it impossible for me to stay focused on the people at the bar. Especially when the voice in my head piped up.

They're gossiping about you, Michael.

I was right back to being the kid getting bullied at school.

Remember how you dealt with that? the voice said. *That's how we're going to deal with this. Stuck-up cunts. They think they're better than you. They think they can push you around. Let them have it, Michael. Let them have it!*

With a pint glass in my hand, I marched over to where my office enemies were standing and asked one of the women – her name was Linda – straight out.

'What did you just say about me?'

She looked taken aback.

'I don't know what you're talking about,' she said. 'We're not talking about you.'

I didn't believe her.

'You've got a problem with me, haven't you?' I said.

'Don't be ridiculous.'

'I'm not stupid,' I told her. 'You're always talking about me behind my back.'

The woman denied it, of course, but all the resentment that had been building up over the past few months suddenly erupted. I called her every name under the sun, getting right in her face. The woman gave as good as she was getting, screaming back at me and waving her bottle at me threateningly. It wasn't long before the whole party was watching us row. Then one of the guys tried to intervene and I started on him too.

'Do you want it, mate? Do you?'

It was seconds away from becoming a full-on fight when the boss intervened. He physically parted me from Linda's knight in shining armour. While Linda was comforted by her horrified friends, he took me into another room.

The boss sat me down at a table and asked me what on earth was going on.

When I told him about the women from the office, he seemed to understand.

'We can't expect to get along with everybody,' he said.

219

'Hopefully you and Linda will sort things out when you're back in the office, but for now I think you need a moment or two to calm down. Stay there while I get you a drink.'

If my colleagues didn't know I was an alcoholic, my boss certainly didn't. Perhaps he thought that getting me another drink might help me mellow out. He returned to the table with a couple of large brandies. One for him and one for me. He toasted me.

'Here's to my top salesman.'

I knocked my brandy back. And then I had another. And another. My boss kept setting the brandies up and I kept drinking them until finally I had a blackout.

It's hard to describe what those blackouts were like. I wasn't unconscious. I was still drinking, talking, maybe even laughing, until suddenly I wasn't. But I lost a whole period of time that I've never since been able to recover. I don't know what I did or said between the third brandy and the next time I was even vaguely aware of what I was doing, which was pinning my boss down in a chokehold out on the tarmac in the car park.

'Michael!' someone yelled at me. 'Let him go!'

People were pouring out of the hotel to see what was going on. There was screaming and yelling. I held my boss to the ground like he was a demon and I was the only thing stopping him from killing everyone around. I would not let him go. His hands scrabbled at my arm around his neck, getting weaker and weaker as I choked the life out of him. I didn't know what on earth had sparked me off but I wasn't going to stop until one of us was dead.

'Michael!'

It took two blokes to pull me off him. They dragged me a safe distance away and held me with my arms behind my back. My boss lay coughing and spluttering on the ground. He held his hands to his throat and gasped for air. He was soon surrounded by people trying to help him up.

'What the hell happened?' people wanted to know.

I had no idea.

'It's OK,' my boss managed to say. 'I'm OK.'

'Should we call the police?' someone asked.

'No,' said my boss. 'Somebody just get him home.'

Two of my colleagues supported the boss and took him back inside. I was still in the car park, being restrained by two men. I shook them off. I was ranting about Linda and her mates, blaming them for what had happened. I didn't even know what had happened. I was making no sense at all.

There was a taxi nearby, waiting for guests going home. When it was clear that I was in deep shit, I jumped into the taxi and said, 'Drive.'

I should have gone straight home but instead I asked to be taken to the other end of town. To Hayley's manager Ciara's house, which was where I thought Hayley would have ended up after their party. The taxi driver dropped me off and drove away before I could change my mind.

The house was dark but I still hammered on the door and somehow convinced myself that there were people inside. They were hiding from me. They'd switched the lights off when they saw me coming, hadn't they? I convinced myself that Hayley was in there and she was laughing at me from behind the closed curtains. She'd told her mates not to let me in because I was drunk and I might pick a fight.

'Hayley!' I pounded on the door with both fists. Still nothing. 'Bitch,' I spat. 'I know you're in there.'

And I was determined to catch her out. I went round the back of the house and broke in. I smashed a pane of glass in the back door, put my hand through and opened it. I crept into the kitchen. I was still sure that there were people in the house somewhere. They were hiding in another room. I threw open door after door, thinking I would take them by surprise.

Of course, there was no one there. Ciara's house was empty but for me. But instead of cutting my losses and leaving, I decided to sit down and wait. Hayley would be back soon. If she came back with a bloke, I would be there to greet them.

Anticipating a long wait, I went to the fridge. There were twelve beers and a bottle of vodka. I helped myself. I drank several beers at the kitchen table then I carried the vodka upstairs, where I got undressed and got into Ciara's bed. I drank half the vodka before I lay down and passed out.

In the early hours of the morning, Ciara and her boyfriend Connor, whose beer I had been drinking, came home alone. Everyone else who'd been at the party had gone back to their respective houses. They soon found the broken pane of glass in the door and empty beer cans all over the kitchen floor. Of course, they assumed they'd been burgled. Connor armed himself with a kitchen knife and searched downstairs. But then Ciara found a pair of shoes, placed neatly at the bottom of the stairs. Drunk as I was, I hadn't wanted to get dirt on the clean white carpet.

Telling Ciara to stay safely in the kitchen, Connor climbed up quietly to see who was in the house. He found me sleeping in the bed like a big ugly Goldilocks, without the hair.

'It's only fucking Michael.'

Connor got Ciara to call Hayley, who begged them to just let me sleep it off, not knowing what I would do if I was woken up before I wanted to be, and at least if I was asleep I wasn't drinking. To their credit, Connor and Ciara agreed to Hayley's plan. They would sleep in the spare room and deal with me the following morning.

I woke up a couple of hours later. It was 4 a.m. and I didn't have a clue where I was or how I got there. I couldn't even find a light. I felt my way out of the bedroom and managed to find the toilet. Staring in the mirror, I asked myself, *What have you done this time?* I was still drunk. I thought perhaps I was still dreaming.

Then in the semi-darkness I walked downstairs, and seeing my shoes at the bottom of the stairs, exactly where I'd left them, I remembered everything.

'Fuck.'

Needless to say, when Ciara and Connor woke up, they didn't offer me any breakfast.

When I got home, I could tell that Hayley had been crying. Really crying. First my birthday weekend in Isleworth, then Jamaica and now this. I'd broken into her boss's house. Though I'd offered to pay for the damage and tried to clear up the mess, Hayley was sure she was going to lose her job over my latest bender.

'Why do you have to be such an idiot?' Hayley wailed.

I did my best to apologize but Hayley didn't want to hear anything I had to say. 'You said you wouldn't drink,' she reminded me.

223

'I said I'd have a couple.'

'A couple of dozen? How drunk do you have to be to break into your girlfriend's boss's house and then get into her bed? What on earth made you think that was a good idea?'

I couldn't remember. The whole evening had fragmented in my mind like a broken mirror. I saw only flashes. A beer. A face. The taxi. Trying to piece it back together was impossible. Hayley kept crying. When I tried to put my arm around her to comfort her, she shook me off.

'I will never forgive you for this.'

As it happened, Ciara and Connor were remarkably understanding. When Hayley spoke to Ciara again, Ciara said that they would keep the whole affair between them. No one else needed to know. It wasn't Hayley's fault. And they were trying their best to believe it wasn't my fault either. Hayley told them I knew I had a problem. She told about the meetings I'd been going to and how well I'd been doing prior to that night. This was a one-off. Ciara said she understood. She wished me luck.

'What exactly happened at your work party?' Hayley asked me later that day, while I quietly nursed the hangover I deserved.

The truth was, I really wasn't sure.

And because I really wasn't sure what I'd done, I went into work on Monday as though nothing had happened at all. My boss hadn't called the police so perhaps I really hadn't been that bad. But as I stepped into reception, the woman on the front desk actually gasped. She rang for security, thinking I must be back to finish what I'd started on Friday night.

'You can't go in,' she said.

A large number of my colleagues quickly gathered in reception, ready to see what happened next. What happened next was my boss, whose face was grazed and bruised from having kissed the tarmac on Friday night, came out of his office and invited me in for a 'talk'.

'I think everybody is a bit surprised to see you here, Michael,' he said. 'After Friday.'

'I'm sorry I shouted at Linda,' I said. 'I'll make sure I apologize to her.'

'That's good. But you don't remember what happened after you argued with Linda?' my boss asked me.

I had to admit that I didn't. Not clearly.

He filled me in. I felt hot and cold as I heard the details. As he recounted my pinning him down in a chokehold, he subconsciously pulled at his collar.

'I am so *so* sorry,' I said.

'I'm sure you are. Look, Michael, I think we both know you can't keep working here anymore. I've got to let you go. But more than that, Michael. I think you need professional help.'

I walked out of the office with the eyes of all my former colleagues on my back. I could hear them whispering and this time I knew for sure that they were all talking about me. I was just lucky that my boss had decided against making a criminal matter of the whole thing.

It was almost Christmas again. The windows of the houses on the street where we lived opened onto Christmas trees, glittering with fairy lights, full of promise for the festival ahead. But my heart was cold and dark as I walked home to our empty place. Hayley was at work, at the job I'd jeopardized. I dreaded her coming home and having to tell her the full story about

Friday night and how it led to me being unemployed yet again. What choice would she have but to leave me now?

How many times had I promised her I would get sober? How many times had I let her down? I felt like the lowest piece of scum on the earth. And I realized that the only thing that stopped me from feeling that way was taking another drink. I opened the fridge. There was nothing there.

I sat on the sofa and waited for Hayley to come home. I didn't even turn the lights on. I just sat there and waited for the inevitable. I didn't deserve Hayley, I never had, and now I was going to lose her.

'You need professional help.' I played my boss's parting shot over in my mind. But I'd had professional help. I'd had all those sessions with David the therapist. I'd been to all those meetings. And I was still an alcoholic.

I thought of Mum, sitting on the bench with her alkie mates. I thought of Dad, weaving down the street with a can of Holsten, on his way to buy heroin. I was just like them. Nothing could change the way I was. I was fundamentally broken. Had been from the start. Always would be. Addiction was in my bones.

When Hayley got home and found me on the sofa, she knew at once what must have happened. She took it surprisingly calmly.

'You just have to go back to the meetings,' she said.

28

I didn't want to but I went to a meeting that very night. To the outside, it looked as though I was taking Hayley's advice, my boss's advice, Mum's advice, and the advice of all the people I'd met in that meeting. I was starting over. But inside I was angry. My self-pity had turned to rage and now I was turning it outwards.

It wasn't my fault that I had got drunk at the Christmas party. It was the fault of the women at work who'd made me feel like I couldn't get through an evening in their company without a drink in my hand. It was the fault of my boss, who kept on plying me with brandy when I was obviously already too far gone. It was the fault of Hayley for not being at Ciara's house when I turned up there. It was Ciara and Connor's fault for having alcohol in their fridge where I could find it. It was Mum's fault, for not starting her own recovery when it might have made a difference to my childhood. It was the fault of the regime at Feltham, which didn't give me the support I needed. It was Dad's fault, for walking out on me when I was too small to understand why.

With all these people behind me, was it any surprise that I ended up drunk and unemployed all the time? I was furious with the hand I'd been dealt.

So I turned up at that meeting full of anger that needed to be expressed and passed on. I was determined to make it the problem of the people I would see there. As soon as the meeting was open, I took the floor.

'You're wasting your time,' I told them. 'This shit doesn't work. I've listened to you all going on for months on end and I've done everything the book tells me to and I still can't stop drinking.' I threw my copy of the twelve-step book across the room. 'It's bullshit. All of this. I've tried and now I'm giving up.'

Around the circle, more than a couple of people had their heads in their hands as they listened to me rant about why the twelve-step programme was just a massive con and how I wasn't going to waste another minute on sitting in that stinking room listening to their hard-luck stories. It wasn't helping me. It couldn't possibly be helping them either.

'You're a bunch of mugs. It's all brainwashing and I ain't ready to be brainwashed,' I said.

But I didn't storm out. I sat back down. I was still there, still wanting someone to tell me that it could be different. I was choked up, though I managed to hold back from breaking down. Only one tear escaped but I didn't think anyone saw it. Then the meeting ended and people began to file out into the night.

I got up to leave. My rant hadn't made me feel any better. Someone tried to give me back my book. I shrugged them off. I didn't want it.

'I'm going down the pub,' I said, making everyone within earshot wince.

It was then that Sean took me by the arm. He had seen that single tear.

'Hang on, Michael,' he said. 'Come back and sit here with me for just a minute.'

There was something about the way he said it that made me decide I would give him that minute.

Sean sat me down beside him in the emptying room.

'I listened to everything you said back there,' he told me. 'And I get it. I really do. I could see the desperation behind your anger. You feel let down and I understand why. You've been coming to all these meetings but you're not getting any better, right? But maybe there's a way to do things differently. You haven't been working the steps, have you? While you were speaking, Michael, I asked God for guidance, and the guidance I got was that I should take you through the first three steps myself. If you'll let me.'

I stared at Sean. What he was offering was more valuable than he could possibly know. He was right. I hadn't been working the steps because I didn't think I needed to. I hadn't tried asking for a sponsor either.

The rules of the twelve-step programme were that if you wanted a sponsor you had to ask for one yourself, and I hadn't dared because, deep down, I didn't think that anyone would really want to take me on. Yet here was Sean breaking rank and offering me the help I was too afraid to ask for.

'Yes, please,' I said in a small voice.

'Good man,' said Sean, patting me on the shoulder. 'Coming to the meetings is one thing but in my experience it's working the steps that really makes the difference. We can start whenever you're ready.'

I realized I finally was.

*

Sean reaching out to me was the first step on the road to sanity. He was there for me all the way. He listened. He truly listened. He made me realize that I did still have a choice. Sean himself had been in recovery for thirty years. He knew what he was talking about. It wasn't going to be easy but if I dedicated myself to the process, it would definitely work.

The day after the meeting where Sean said he would sponsor me, we began the process.

Step one. I admitted that I was powerless over alcohol and that my life had become unmanageable.

After the Christmas party disaster I could no longer pretend that alcohol was not a problem for me. The idea that I could continue to drink – sticking to just one or two – was a fairy tale. I had known what would happen if I drank at the Christmas party. I didn't want the chaos and the consequences and yet I had still gone ahead and ordered that first beer. That's powerless right there.

Sean broke the step down for me in a language I understood. He explained to me that, even though I'd managed a long spell without drinking, when things got difficult I'd reached for the alcohol again. That was life being unmanageable. I couldn't look after myself.

Sean also pointed out to me that I didn't know how to properly look after myself because I'd never been shown by my parents, who hadn't been shown by their parents and on and on back through the generations.

'But we are going to break the cycle,' he promised me.

Step one was easy. I was more than ready to admit I was powerless. Step two was a little harder to get my head around.

'We came to believe that a Power greater than ourselves could restore us to sanity.'

The first part of this sentence was fine. Though I didn't believe in the man in the sky with the big white beard that my years as a child in the Catholic Church had conjured up for me, I did believe there was something out there. A life force, an energy, Mother Nature, or even just good energy from other human beings. And I knew when I was fucked, really fucked, I did pray to 'God', whatever it was, and I knew I felt some hope when I did so. It was the second part of the sentence than stuck in my throat. To be 'restored to sanity', you had to first admit you were insane.

Wasn't 'insane' another word for mad? I was angry. I was desperate. But I didn't think I was mad. No way would I cop to that.

Again, Sean explained the step in terms I might finally understand. If I was going to progress, then I had to let go of my prejudices around the word 'insanity'.

'It's like this,' said Sean. 'Insanity is doing the same thing again and again and expecting a different result.'

It was a lightbulb moment. Wasn't that the story of my life? I'd been doing the same things over and over again. Drinking to avoid feeling. Knowing that it would lead to chaos yet still hoping against hope that getting drunk would actually help me escape my uncomfortable emotions. My thinking was insanity. I was at once elated that I'd worked out the problem but overwhelmed with the idea of actually fixing it.

'You don't have to tackle this alone,' Sean reassured me. 'With the help of your higher power – whatever that is to you – we can work towards a sane way of living.'

As we worked towards step three, I felt hopeful. Step three instructed that we 'turned our will and our life over to the care of God as we understood Him'.

'This is where you take action,' Sean explained. 'You have to hand over to your higher power. Your willpower has failed you again and again so now you need to ask for your God's help to direct your thinking from now on.'

In Sean's living room, he and I kneeled down together in front of a candle and read the step three prayer.

Looking down at my hands, I saw that I was shaking. I wondered if Sean knew that this was the most intimate moment I had shared with a man in my life. Never before had a man taken such an interest in my well-being and made a space where I could relax and trust.

Sean worked hard to make sure that I knew I could trust him absolutely, but I was still scared I was going to get hurt. I was praying for help, but at the same time my head was full of memories of Tommy and what had happened with him, and how he and the Catholic Church between them had convinced me that I was going to hell for the sins I'd committed or somehow made other people commit.

God wasn't going to listen to me. The God I'd been raised to believe in was busy going through that long list of things I'd done wrong. Why should he try to help?

The voice in my head was loud, but for the moment Sean's voice was louder. He read the prayer and I repeated the words after him.

'God, I offer myself to Thee – to build with me and to do with me as Thou wilt, relieve me of the bondage of self, that I may better do Thy will, take away my difficulties, that victory over them may bear witness to those I would help of Thy Power, Thy Love and Thy Way of Life.'

With the prayer spoken, I opened my eyes and looked at the candle flame, flickering in a draught.

I had been half expecting a thunderbolt. For the clouds to part and a finger to point right at me while a voice boomed, 'Michael, you're still a worthless shit.' Of course, nothing happened. There was just me and Sean and silence.

After a moment, Sean leaned over to me and gave me a hug and I realized I felt peaceful. It was a peace like I hadn't felt in a long time, a feeling like I wasn't alone, a feeling like I had come home.

So, I was working the steps at last. Really working them. I had another job, with a company called Speedy Hire. I seemed to be getting my life back on track. But meanwhile something strange was happening at home. While every day I was feeling better about myself and more convinced that I could finally beat this thing called alcoholism, my relationship with Hayley was beginning to deteriorate.

Hayley had been by my side for seven years. She had seen me at my very worst and always told me she was sticking by me because she knew I could get better. Yet, here I was, getting better, and Hayley didn't seem half as excited about it as I'd hoped she might be. Somehow, without the drama of my getting drunk and crazy to distract us, the real differences between us were starting to show up.

Now that I was working the steps with Sean, I was being much more careful about not putting myself in situations where I would be tempted to backslide. That meant that I wasn't up for going out as much as I used to be. Hayley said she didn't mind, but I worried that she found it boring staying in night after night. She still went out with her friends from work and when she came back it was clear she'd had a few drinks. I tried not to mind but of course I wished she wouldn't.

It was as though we were on the ends of a see-saw and we couldn't find a balance. When I was drinking, Hayley was the sensible one. Now I wasn't drinking, it was as though Hayley was trying to find a way to bring the excitement and drama back.

I had been sober for eight months when I realized that we couldn't continue in this way. Hayley's sister and cousin were visiting us in Belfast. They were all sitting around in the living room, drinking shots and laughing. For a horrible moment I felt the way I'd felt in Jamaica and again at the Christmas party. I was on the outside looking in. They were having fun without me. If I just had a couple of shots, I would feel so much better. I'd feel like part of the gang again. I had the feeling that Hayley wouldn't have tried to stop me.

It took an enormous effort to stand up and walk away. While they carried on drinking, I went to the bedroom and called Sean. It was late, but he didn't mind. He said he was glad I'd chosen talking to him over taking that drink.

'But you need to talk to Hayley,' he said. 'What you're dealing with is hard enough without feeling like she doesn't get it.'

As soon as her sister and cousin were gone, I spoke to her. I told her that I was finding it too difficult to stop drinking when she wouldn't. I told her I knew I couldn't ask her to. But my recovery had to take priority for me now. There didn't seem to be any option but to break up.

We talked late into the night, trying to find a compromise, but the truth was Hayley knew I was right. I was trying so hard to change. I was weak and she was constantly putting temptation in my way by continuing to party like we used to. Eventually, we agreed we had to part. Hayley moved back to London while I stayed in Ireland in the house we'd made our home.

After she'd gone, I sat in the house on my own wondering what I'd done. Drink and drugs had already taken so much from me. My childhood had been tainted by Mum's drinking. My adolescence had been ruined by decisions I'd made under the influence. I'd lost jobs and friends. I'd put myself in danger. I thought that finally admitting I had a problem and making a serious effort to deal with it would be the beginning of better times. Instead, I was having to say goodbye to the woman I loved. The woman who had stood by me when I was at my very worst. It just didn't seem fair.

Of course, I talked to Sean about it and he did his best to convince me that it was worth the trade-off.

But without Hayley, I couldn't hack Ireland on my own for long. Apart from the people I met at the meetings, I didn't really have friends there. People like Kyle and Trisha belonged to a different life. Our friendship had been based around partying.

By this time I was working for Speedy Hire. They had branches all over place. When a job came up at Heathrow, I jumped at the opportunity and moved back to the UK.

29

Sean, who had guided me so carefully through the first three steps, warned me that I should make sure I had support in London right from the beginning. I quickly found a new meeting to go to and wasted no time in asking for a new sponsor. The first man to step up was Matt. Matt was a successful businessman. He would go far beyond the role of sponsor, becoming more of an all-round life coach to me. Now that I was no longer drinking and could start to see something of a future, I knew I wanted some of his brand of success.

By this time, I was up to step four, which meant I promised to make a 'searching and fearless moral inventory of myself'.

It was not an easy thing to do. Since quitting drink again, I'd realized that I had spent a lot of my life making excuses for myself. That's what they were. Excuses. Sure, I hadn't had the best start in life. Mum and Dad were both ill-equipped to be parents. Their neglect – wilful or not – had definitely caused me a lot of problems but I was an adult now and it was time to take the responsibility for my decisions and choices onto my own shoulders. Plenty of kids had a bad start in life. Not all of them went on to become career criminals as I had. Not all of them turned to drugs and drink.

While I hadn't known unconditional love and support, I had always known right from wrong.

The people I'd hurt during my years as a robber, a burglar and a drug dealer were constantly at the forefront of my mind when I returned to London. For so long I'd convinced myself that the crimes I committed were just a small matter of balancing the scales. Those people in Richmond whose houses I burgled had everything; I had nothing. Those people in the shops I robbed, they could get their stock back in insurance. It wouldn't cost them anything in the end. Those people I sold drugs to were buying from me of their own free will. If they didn't buy from me, they'd just go somewhere else. I'd have been a fool not to take their money, right?

Now, however, I finally started to understand the damage I had caused and I felt ashamed. Properly ashamed. I remembered the terrified faces of the people who had been at the wrong end of my anger. I remembered the old lady in the corner shop. How many sleepless nights had I given her? I remembered Arthur, the paperboy, whose only mistake was to be in the wrong place at the wrong time. I'd wanted him to pay for grassing on me. Had I left him too scared to walk down the streets where he'd grown up? Did the people I'd burgled ever feel safe in their homes again? I had undoubtedly ruined many lives.

Now that I was forcing myself to think about the consequences of all my mistakes, I thought the guilt would overwhelm me. But it was all I deserved because I'd taken my pain and turned it into everyone else's problem.

Working the steps was getting tougher. Having to look at my past through sober eyes, there were moments when reaching for a beer or a spliff definitely seemed preferable. Always at the end of the phone when I needed him, Matt reassured me all the way.

'We are building an arch through which you could walk a free man. Don't be too hard on yourself. Remember you are doing this to clean up your side of the street and make restitution for harm done. And to heal the harm that was done to you.'

It took me a long time to write it all down. On several occasions, I was overwhelmed with sadness and guilt and shame and had to put the inventory aside. However, when it was finally done and Matt and I went through it together, I felt a huge sense of relief. I felt like at least one person finally knew the whole truth about me and hadn't used it against me or walked away from me because of it. Matt still wanted to be my mentor. He told me he was proud of me for getting this far and slowly, slowly, my belief that the universe wasn't a friendly place started to change. I began to think maybe there was a place for me in this world.

Now that I'd looked at the past as carefully as I could and admitted to myself with honesty what I'd done and the harm I'd caused as a result, I wanted to make up for it.

One of the first steps my new mentor Matt helped me navigate is a process called 'making amends'. It's when you apologize to all those people whose lives have been affected by your addiction and it's one of the most difficult steps to undertake. I had a long list of apologies to make, starting with my family. But apologizing to Mum and Pete, and Maria, Sophie and Justin, was going to be easy compared with some of the amends I had to make. As I wrote down the long list of names of people I'd wronged – at least those I could remember – I felt my heart drop at the scale of the task I had before me.

Two incidences from that time stand out in particular. The first was the apology I made to a man called Louis.

Back when I was running wild as a teenager in Isleworth, I had a friend called Jordan. Jordan was feral like I was. I sold drugs for his dad. When Jordan went to trial on a manslaughter charge, there was only one witness. His name was Louis. He'd grown up alongside us. I might even have called him a mate at one time. Anyway, Louis testified and Jordan went to prison.

On the day of Jordan's sentencing, I was over at his dad's house, smoking and drinking. When I heard what had happened, I swore revenge on Jordan's behalf. Nobody got away with grassing on one of my friends. Together with some other lads, I went to Louis' house that night, dragged him out into the front garden and beat him in front of his family, who could only stand there until it was time to call an ambulance. I left them in no doubt that calling the police would be a big mistake.

Where did I start to apologize for that? To begin with, I wasn't even sure I would. The caveat to the amends process is that you should only do it where to do so won't cause further harm. I doubted that Louis would be pleased to see me. I agonized over Louis for weeks until I was sure that to apologize to him could only be a good thing.

The first thing I had to do was to find out where Louis was living. He had moved away from his parents' house which is where I'd found him after Jordan's trial. Possibly because he feared more repercussions to his testifying at the murder trial. I tried to track Louis down online but found nothing. I talked to Matt, who told me firmly that I shouldn't turn it into a stalking exercise. If I couldn't find Louis, I couldn't find him. I should leave it up to chance. I grudgingly agreed.

The very next day, I saw Louis' mum coming out of a shop. I didn't approach her right away. She really had no reason to be happy to see my face again. But I followed her at a distance and as I did so, I realized that it wasn't just Louis to whom I needed to make amends. It was his whole family. When Louis' mum went into her house, I waited a while and then I knocked. She appeared at the door, which remained on the latch, flanked by her entire family.

She must have known I was following her and she looked appalled to see me on her doorstep. She knew exactly who I was. She'd known me since I was a child. Behind her, her husband and kids bristled with hostility. If I'd come to make trouble, they weren't having it.

'You get away from us,' her husband said.

I had to beg for an audience.

'I know you've got no reason to want to listen to me, after what I did, but I'm not here to give you grief. I'm here because I want you to know I'm doing everything I can not to be that person you knew anymore.'

They looked confused and suspicious, as they had every right to be.

'Please. I'm not the person you used to know. I'm in recovery. I'm trying to change my life. I only came here to apologize.'

Louis' mum's face softened just a little.

'To apologize?'

'Yes.'

It turned out Louis wasn't there. But he wasn't the only member of the family I had to say sorry to anyway.

The latch was taken off the door but I was still left to stand on the step. Louis' whole family watched me closely as I took them through all that had happened to me since they last saw me. The time I'd spent in prison. Ireland. How I'd come to realize that I had a problem with addiction. How I wanted to be a better man now and admitting my past mistakes was an important part of that.

I felt sweat gathering on my forehead as I went through the speech I'd been preparing for weeks. How were they taking it? Maybe this was mad, thinking that they'd want an apology from me.

'I'm truly sorry for the way I behaved,' I ended my spiel. 'I was a little shit.'

There was silence for a moment or two. I wanted to jump up and run, but I knew that I owed them the right of reply. It seemed like an age before Louis' mother reached for my hand.

'We knew you were a good boy underneath, Michael. When you were younger, you always stood up for the little kids. And we knew you had it hard with your dad gone and your mum drinking like she did.'

I nodded. 'But I'm not using that as an excuse anymore,' I told her. 'I knew what I was doing was wrong.'

I didn't stay much longer. It didn't seem appropriate. Though the atmosphere on the doorstep had improved dramatically, I knew I wasn't exactly a welcome guest. I wasn't going to be invited in for tea.

As I left, Louis' mum gave me a spontaneous hug. I struggled to hold on to my tears as she held me in her warm arms.

'You take care,' she said. 'Good luck.'

For the first time in my life, I felt something approaching pride. I felt love. And I felt relief. I never had to be that guy I was ashamed of again.

Making amends for what I'd done to Louis was an uplifting and freeing experience. His family had taken my apology at face value and that meant more than I had imagined. (And four years ago, I bumped into Louis himself and we hugged it out in person.) But not everybody was so pleased to see me.

Around the same time that I was seeking revenge on behalf of Jordan, I'd robbed a house. Unlike my usual strategy, it wasn't a house belonging to an unlucky stranger. It was a house belonging to someone I knew very well. A rival drug dealer. It was a crazy move but at the time I was thinking only about where my next heroin fix would come from. So I turned this bloke's house over and he knew that I'd done it. The only thing that kept him from killing me was the fact that I had bigger and better friends than he did back then.

I was ticking off the names on my amends list at quite a speed. Now I came to the dealer. Did I really have to say sorry to him? He wasn't what anyone would have called an 'innocent victim'. Mentally, I tried to wriggle myself out of it, but Matt put me straight. I hadn't gone to the dealer's house and evened up any kind of score. I'd taken things that were personal to him as well as drugs. He needed an apology.

I soon tracked him down on Facebook and sent him a message, saying I'd like the opportunity to say 'sorry' to his face. I don't know what sort of response I'd expected but I was hoping it would go the same way as it had with Louis' mum.

I was still high on the way that had made me feel and – ever the addict – I was keen for another hit of approval.

A reply came quickly.

'If I see you, Maisey, it's fucking on. This beef is never squashed.'

I had my response prepared. Matt had taken me through the possibility that someone would find my efforts unwelcome.

'I hear you,' I wrote, 'and I'm sad you feel that way. I just wanted you to know that I'm sorry for what I did.'

The next message was almost instant.

'Come near me or anyone who knows me and you are fucking dead.'

They say that words can never hurt you but I knew that this particular bloke could definitely back them up. I stared at the screen, reading the last message over and over, feeling my insides go liquid as I realized I still had a serious enemy and I'd unwittingly let him know where I was. Shit. What was I going to do if I saw him? What if he saw me first?

My street instincts kicked in and I decided I needed a gun. A real gun this time. Not like the replica that had got me into trouble all those years before. I went into panic mode. I couldn't risk coming face to face with this bloke. He was a man who always made good on his promises.

By the time I found Matt and explained what had happened, I was convinced I was a dead man walking. I told Matt why I needed a weapon. He just laughed.

'God hasn't saved you from drowning to kick the shit out of you on the beach,' was his response to my panic. Just as he'd told me when I complained about not being able to find Louis, I had to leave this one up to fate. I couldn't force people to react to my making amends the way I wanted them to. I could only offer my words of apology and hope they were heard in the way I intended them to be heard. The situation with Louis had worked out for the best. This new situation looked bad, Matt agreed, but I didn't need a weapon. I needed faith.

Everything, every one of the steps I had worked through so far, led back to the same thing. I had to have faith. That was how it worked. Trusting in my higher power was how I would walk the walk. So I didn't get hold of a gun and I never saw the dealer again.

From January to May of 2009, I spent my time making amends. I had a lot of amends to make. It was one of the hardest of the steps, requiring me to be humble and trusting, two ways of being I had spent my life trying to avoid. Being humble marked you out as a victim. Being trusting was for mugs. Yet I was being asked to be both. It required a complete change of outlook. I had to look at the world in an entirely different way, undoing years of learning that dog-eat-dog was the way of the world. The armour I had been wearing since I was a child had to be taken off and melted down and shaped into a new heart.

Matt also guided me through the next three steps. Step ten commanded that 'we continued to take personal inventory and when we were wrong promptly admitted it.' Matt explained that this meant I had to check in every day with how I was feeling and quickly correct any wrong thinking or behaviour. Step eleven was to look to my spiritual growth. Step twelve was to see how I might help others.

Helping others was something that suddenly appealed to me. Previously, I'd been too focused on helping myself. In May 2009, I ran the London Marathon. I committed to a training plan and raised loads of money in sponsorship. I finished the course in five hours and ten minutes. When I crossed the finish line, I felt invincible. Completing the marathon gave me a sense of personal power that I could never get from owning a gun. It also proved another set of fears wrong. I had been using alcohol and drugs from the age of twelve. I had treated my body like a walking dustbin. I'd filled my lungs and liver with every poison imaginable and yet my body carried me for twenty-six miles. I was astonished and humbled that I made it all the way.

My friends and family turned out to watch me that day. And Hayley. Hayley was there too. When I saw her standing there at the finish line, looking at me with tears in her eyes, my newly built heart leapt out to her. Hayley, my first real love and my best friend.

I didn't realize until that moment just how much I had been missing her. I told her I was glad to see her and I meant it.

Later that day, Hayley and I got together for a talk. She told me that she'd been missing me too. Halfway through the evening, Hayley admitted that she wondered if there was any chance we could get back together. When I responded that I was still too fragile to be around her if she was living the way she had in Belfast, she promised me that she would stop partying if that's what it took so that we could be together. I meant so much to her, she would do whatever she had to, she promised. She wanted to be with me more than she needed the party life.

By the end of the conversation, we had agreed to give our relationship another try. Not having Hayley around had been hard for me. I trusted her and I was sure that, now she really understood what I needed, we could make both our relationship and my recovery work.

30

A few weeks after we rekindled our relationship, Hayley and I rented a place together in Sunbury. We were both working. I went to meetings. Matt continued to mentor me, guiding me towards a personal development programme, Anthony Robbins' Personal Power II, which he hoped would help me to pull together my working life. I had some business ideas that Matt thought might have some legs, one of which was setting up my own tool-hire company, similar to the company I'd been working for. He said he was willing to invest in me if I came up with the right business plan. With Matt's backing, I felt as though everything was coming together at last.

It was around this time that I met Luke at a men's meeting. We clicked immediately. I sensed that he was living the kind of life I wanted for myself and I was determined to learn everything I could from him. Luke was around four years older than me. He was a big guy, with a rugby player's build. He was into body-building. He had a successful business. And he was married with two kids, who he was there for in a real way. He was a good partner, a good dad, a good ethical businessman . . . And he was sober. Like Matt, he understood that I was ambitious and said he'd read my business plan when it was ready. Before then, he had other ideas for me.

'It's time for you to chair a meeting,' he said.

The idea was daunting. Though I regularly spoke up at meetings now, I wasn't sure I could actually chair one. There were so many serious, intelligent men at the meetings we attended. I didn't want to let them down.

'Not here,' said Luke. 'At Feltham.'

'Feltham Young Offenders?'

'Where else?'

It was a big moment for me. I was twenty-seven years old. I had been sober for sixteen months, having not had a drink since that terrible night at the Christmas party in Belfast back in 2007. Yet I still did not feel ready to share my experience. Let alone in Feltham. The very word made me feel sick inside.

'You're the perfect man for this,' said Luke. 'You've been there. You understand what it's like to be inside.'

I couldn't tell him that it was precisely because I understood that I didn't want to go back there. I still felt like a work in progress and I worried that the memories that being back in that place would drag up might unravel all the good stuff I'd been doing. I already felt strange and sad as I considered the idea. But Luke wasn't going to let me off easily. He reminded me of the twelfth step. Helping other people. This was an opportunity for me to make a big impact, he said. There were kids in there who *needed* to hear from me. They needed to hear that someone understood, that there was someone who really knew what their lives were like.

'Just as you needed to hear it, but didn't. Imagine if you had. You're always saying how different your life could have been if you'd had more support to get sober earlier. You could save some of these kids from going through everything you've been through,' Luke said. 'Isn't that worth the risk?'

'But what will I say?'

'Just tell them what it's been like for you. Don't dress it up. Tell it like it is. If it helps even one of them, it will be worth it.'

He had me convinced.

When I told Hayley what Luke was suggesting, she gave me a hug.

'You'll be brilliant,' she said. She thought it was a great idea.

'I wish you could come with me.'

But there was no question of that.

'I'll be thinking of you all the time you're in there,' Hayley promised me. 'I'm so proud of you, Michael. This is a great opportunity.'

I started to see it as such. But as the day of the meeting drew near, I couldn't help but get nervous again. I was going back to Feltham. It seemed impossible that I had ever been excited about the place. How naive I'd been as a sixteen-year-old, sitting in the back of the prison van with Ivan, imagining how my credibility on the street would be off the scale when we got out. Now I knew what it was really like and the memories came tumbling through my head like jump cuts from a horror movie.

I remembered squatting in the reception area while the guard checked my anus. I saw the hate on Pepsi's face at that first fight in the shower. I saw Jeremy's cold white feet as the guards carried his corpse past my cell. I saw Pepsi again, leering as his mates punched me until I passed out. I saw the ceiling of that first cell on Wren wing, as I rolled from the bed and the blanket rope tightened around my neck. Remembering all these bad times, the sadness seeped through my body like a poison.

I wasn't much good company in the run-up to the big day. When Hayley said that she would spend the night before the meeting at her mum's place, I was secretly relieved. I wanted to be alone with my thoughts, get my talk prepped and have an early night.

Hayley packed her overnight bag and kissed me goodbye.

The following morning I arrived at Feltham early and was waiting outside when Luke pulled up in a gleaming Ferrari. I had no idea he drove such a flashy car. He grinned as he clambered out. 'You could get one yourself if you work on that business plan of yours.'

But that morning wasn't about Luke's car or my business plan. We had stuff to do.

'Do you know the way in?' he teased me.

'Fuck off,' I said. 'I used to get driven in in an armoured van.'

But though Luke and I were having a joke, I could feel the anxiety rising inside me like a bubble. I was walking back into the scene of the worst days of my life and, just as when I'd arrived there as a teenage prisoner, I didn't feel at all sure that I would be coming out again.

The walk from the car to Wren wing felt like the walk to the scaffold. I was convinced that it was all going to go wrong. As I passed the padded cell where I'd spent three days after my first failed detox and suicide attempt, I could have vomited all over my own feet. The feelings of fear and desperation came back to me so strongly I was shaking as I took my seat in the circle of chairs for the meeting. On the outside, I was doing my best to look in control. On the inside, I was more scared than I had been since I was last on that prison wing for real.

But for all my fears, the meeting went well. After I had finished talking, the kids, who had been so hard to persuade to shut up and listen, actually queued up to shake my hand.

'You've got them all in single file,' one of the guards observed. 'I can never get them to stand in single file.'

I shook hands with each and every one of them. Most of them just wanted to thank me, but some of them wanted to ask me something more. Like Elijah.

'How is this stuff relevant to me?' he asked. 'I mean, it's OK for you to tell us we can get clean but you don't know what I'm going back to. It ain't easy, man. It ain't easy.'

'I know,' I assured him. 'But there is support out there. When you get out, come and find me.'

I told him where I went to meetings.

'Anytime you want to go along, I'll be there.'

'Sure,' he said. 'Thanks.'

He shook my hand and left.

When all the kids were back in their cells, Luke embraced me in a big hug.

'You were amazing,' he said.

I accepted his praise with a shrug. But as we walked back out to the car park, I felt so good I could have danced. I finally felt I'd found my purpose. 'This is why I'm here,' I told Luke. My gift was my story and now that I'd done my first chair I was eager to do more. I couldn't wait to share my revelation with Hayley.

Luke offered me a lift home in the Ferrari but I told him I wanted to walk for a while. I think I wanted to recreate the first time I had walked out of Feltham, when there was no one to meet me so I caught a bus back to Mum's. I wanted to be with that hopeless but ever-hopeful kid who still lived inside me for just a minute or two.

When I was about halfway home, I got my phone out. I knew I had several messages waiting, including one from Hayley. I'd seen it that morning but hadn't listened to it because I was rushing, in a hurry to be at Feltham on time. Now I dialled my voicemail.

Hayley had left her message at three in the morning. It was an odd time to call but I guessed that she'd think I had the phone turned off and just wanted to wish me good luck.

Instead, it soon became obvious that Hayley had not intended to call me at all. She'd accidentally dialled my number and my voicemail had recorded four minutes of her night out. It seemed she'd decided to go clubbing with her mates and, from the sound of her voice, she had had a few drinks. It was fair enough but even so, as I turned off my phone, the euphoria I'd been feeling up until that moment disappeared like smoke on the breeze.

When Hayley got home, we were honest with each other about the fact that our lives were incompatible but neither of us were ready to take that understanding to its logical conclusion. I knew I couldn't bear to say it out loud.

I talked it over with Matt. 'You can't have the life you want in the wrong relationship,' was his view.

Still, I felt that I owed Hayley something. While the way things were right now wasn't serving my recovery, she had been there for me for so long and on so many occasions. I didn't know what I would have done without her, or just the idea of her. How was I going to get along without her now? I couldn't. But I had to. I had to make that choice. Finally, I said what my heart already knew.

'I can't do this anymore.'

Hayley and I said goodbye for the last time.

A week after that meeting in Feltham, Luke called to tell me that he'd read my business plan for setting up a tool-hire company near Heathrow and he loved it. Before breaking up with Hayley, I would have been delighted to hear Luke's view. Now, I just couldn't get excited. Having to let go of Hayley for good had destroyed me. It was taking every bit of energy I had to keep from drinking to make myself feel better. I had to tell Luke that I wasn't in the right place to act on my business plan. Maybe at some point in the future I'd feel differently. He said he understood.

31

So, I was single and I was back in the spare room at Mum's but I was still sober and work for once was actually going well. I'd been promoted to assistant manager at Speedy Hire. I was good at sales. My bosses were pleased with me. I was getting some cash together. But I felt that I needed to do something more. In the spirit of the twelfth step, I thought it should be something that would enable me to help others. I studied to become a therapist, leaving Speedy Hire and volunteering to help people struggling with the issues I'd battled my whole life. I thought I was doing well. People seemed happy to open up to me. However, the place where I volunteered told me I was doing it wrong. I wasn't supposed to disclose my own history to my clients.

I tried to take the criticism on board but the old Michael inside me reacted angrily. I didn't see how I could gain my clients' trust if I couldn't tell them exactly how it was I had come to understand their challenges. Why couldn't I seem to catch a break? I was in that frame of mind as I went to the gym, where I bumped into an old friend from school.

Karl looked in good shape. Better than I remembered. He greeted me warmly and asked how it was going.

'Obviously not as well as it's going for you,' I observed, having seen his fancy watch and heard about his new car. Karl grinned. He was proud of what he'd achieved.

After we'd finished working out, I was open with Karl and told him that I was struggling. I'd tried to change careers but it wasn't going well. Having taken time and money to train myself for a job I wasn't cut out for, I was skint and fed up. I knew that I'd been doing the 'right thing' but I felt like I deserved some of the material things that Karl had for himself. He seemed to read my mind and offered me a solution.

Karl was no businessman. He was a drug dealer. Though he came from a decent family, he'd always idolized the criminal way of life, just as I had once upon a time. He offered me a stash to sell for myself. We'd split the profits. It was a quick way to make a wad of cash.

'And just in time for Christmas.'

I was three years sober. I should have thanked him and moved on. Instead I told him, 'OK.'

It just came out. Something inside me had broken again. My desperation had won the battle between my new ethics and my need for financial security.

When we met up a couple of days later, I took a bunch of coke and sold the lot around a few Christmas parties I'd been invited to. To have the money in my hands again felt good. And I managed not to do any of the coke myself. My customers were happy to buy drugs off someone they trusted. I was pleased to have the cash. Where was the harm?

I told Karl that I would take another ounce.

'Are you fucking joking?' asked my friend Mairead when I confided the truth about my new source of income to her.

'You're in recovery, Michael. You're supposed to be living an honest life. You can't do this. You can't sell the means for someone else to get high. You know what trouble it causes.'

'But . . .'

But I was stuck, was what I was trying to say. I owed Karl now.

'Idiot,' said Mairead.

She marched me to the nearest cash point. There she got out from her own account the same amount of cash I would have made had I sold the drugs. She waved the notes at me then pressed them into my hand.

'Pay me back when you can but I want you to give the drugs back to your friend,' she said. 'And for God's sake don't go near him again.'

I didn't know what to do. It was easy for Mairead to say I should just give the drugs back. She didn't know how these things worked. That night I sat in the living room with Mairead's cash and the drugs side-by-side on the kitchen table and considered my options. I didn't think I had any.

I knew I was a fraud. I knew that I was enabling some of my customers to ruin their lives even while I was supposed to be fixing my own. I stayed awake all night trying to summon up the courage to do what was right.

When I handed the drugs back to Karl the next day, I expected him to be angry but he was only bemused. He didn't understand why I couldn't just do what I'd done before at those Christmas parties. I had a bunch of eager customers. If I was only selling and not using, where was the problem? I wasn't going to get addicted to drugs I wasn't taking, was I? But Mairead was right. This was about more than whether or not

I snorted any of the cocaine I had on me. I was supposed to be living an honest life. Dealing wasn't only dishonest, it was dangerous. I was a man with a serious criminal record. If I was arrested again, I would be going back to prison for sure. All the progress I'd made would be undone. I couldn't go back.

Karl just shook his head.

'Whatever you say, man. Whatever you say.'

Karl couldn't get his mind around my new way of life. He was happy where he was, dealing, dodging the police, showing off the material things that he'd come by dishonestly. He said he understood but I could tell that he thought I was a mug. In Karl's eyes I was choosing the hard path, choosing to suffer for my integrity. He would rather have the car and the watch.

We shook hands and I went home. For a couple of days afterwards, of course, I wondered if I'd done the right thing. I was still skint and now I owed money to Mairead. I couldn't exactly tell any of the employers I was in interviews with that I'd turned down a chance to get rich quick in a drug deal to take their job with its pathetic salary. But gradually I started to be convinced that I'd done the right thing for me. I went to meetings and listened to my fellow addicts talking about how hard it was to change and I was glad that I wasn't part of the system supplying them with the means to stay stuck forever.

Two years later, Karl was killed when a drug deal he was involved in went badly wrong. His body was found on the banks of the Thames. No one was ever convicted of his murder. Karl's death really shook me. It haunted me for months. Because it could have been either one of us.

32

After giving up on my short-lived career as a therapist, I went back to work in sales. This time as an estate agent. I'd met a friend who was working for a local estate agency and he told me they were looking for more staff. I didn't think I had a hope in hell. Didn't people who went to work in a suit have to have a degree or something like that? My friend laughed.

I may have felt like a fraud on the inside but I looked the part and was quickly hired. My history didn't seem to matter. I suppose it wasn't much of a risk for my new bosses. If I didn't hit my targets, I didn't get paid. It was as simple as that.

At first, it seemed impossible that I would be able to reach the targets they set me, but I smashed them. I took on what my new bosses told me then applied everything I had learned from the twelve steps and from Anthony Robbins. And, for once, being in recovery gave me an advantage.

The agency office was full of people my age who lived for Friday night, just like I used to. Now, however, when they went to the pub I went to the gym, and while they were struggling with hangovers I was on top form, and getting the listings and sales they were missing because they felt too ill to properly engage with their clients. It's fair to say that not drinking at the weekends gave me a day and a half on my boozy colleagues.

That translated into weeks of extra time to make my targets. I broke company records in my first year and was asked to train others in how I'd managed it.

I was excited to be making real progress financially at last, but after a while I started to feel a conflict between the need for honesty dictated by the twelve steps and the way the estate-agency business worked. The bad reputation estate agents have with the general public has its roots in some pretty dodgy practice for sure. It wasn't unusual or even uncommon to get a client on board by promising them you could get an unrealistic price for their house. Once they were signed up, most would be too lazy to move when they discovered that the asking price was unachievable. They would let us drop the price and carry on representing them. The price reduction was no big deal to us. A drop in ten grand to the vendor was only a drop of a hundred quid or so in agent's commission.

I didn't like the way it worked. I'd met a lot of great people during my time at the agency. Kind, decent people who deserved to be treated honestly, not lied to for the sake of getting an instruction. I wanted to do things differently. Why not be straightforward from the start, I wondered? Tell people what their place was really worth and then go all out to get that realistic asking price for them instead of wasting their time with pie in the sky numbers they could never hope to get?

I sat down with the directors of the agency and told them what I was thinking. They laughed at me. They told me I was dreaming. The way things were was the way things had been forever. If we didn't promise our clients ridiculous results, they'd just sign up with the next agency that did. I disagreed. I told them you could do the job with integrity. Integrity didn't seem to be a quality that mattered in my office so I handed in my notice.

Fortunately, my old sponsor Matt agreed with me. He'd seen me struggle through the last few steps and knew that I'd embraced the twelve-step system wholeheartedly, just as he had. Matt believed in honesty too and, what's more, he believed in me. He agreed to put money behind my new honest estate agency. I set up the first office in Isleworth and called it Oakhill.

It was a risky move. There were still plenty of people in Isleworth who knew me as the kid who had been in and out of Feltham. A kid who robbed corner shops, burgled houses and wasn't afraid to beat the shit out of anyone who crossed me. And now I was setting up an *honest* estate agency? I understand why it sounded like a joke. In the eyes of many people, I'd just moved from crime to evil, right?

But there were those who believed in me – as Matt did. I had considered setting up outside London or running an online company from home, but I could see that the real opportunity was in Isleworth. I'd made my amends with the locals I'd wronged. My brother Justin told me he was in – he became my first employee. I decided to trust my instincts. The universe responded and on the day I opened the Oakhill office with a party, my Isleworth friends were there in force, willing me to succeed. People like Mary, who'd known me since I was a kid and who had always believed in me and offered me her support and friendship, even when I was in Feltham for the kind of crimes that made her cross herself. Then there were friends from the twelve-step meetings. People who understood that change was possible and even the worst of us deserve a second chance. They were willing me to succeed in proving that I was different from the boy with the gun.

The party was even graced by the local MP, Mary MacLeod. That was surreal. As I posed for photographs with her, I smiled like a lunatic. I must have looked like I was having the time of my life but the whole evening I kept searching the crowd for just a couple of faces. My parents. Mum and my real dad, Kevin. They weren't there and that hurt. Inside I was still the little boy who wanted to make them proud. I think that even then I harboured a secret fantasy that, if they just saw how well I was doing, my family would come together and just be, well, normal. As it was, Mum chose to go to work. None of us had any idea where Kevin was.

After the excitement of the office opening, life settled into a routine. It wasn't all easy. Learning to manage people was a whole new thing for me. I had just about learned to manage myself and my own life. I tried to apply the skills I'd picked up in recovery to my business life, focusing on people's strengths and supporting them in their weaknesses. Sometimes I got it badly wrong.

Financially, it was a struggle to begin with. I'd sold my car to get the money to set the business up. We travelled to viewings in Justin's beat-up Ford Fiesta. He was making minimum wage. I was making nothing at all. I remember one month when I had four full-time members of staff to pay on the 31st but by the 28th I had just £990 in the bank. Somehow we scraped by. I was working twelve-hour days, seven days a week, doing all I could. There were moments when I wondered what the hell I was doing and considered giving up. Rival companies were offering me good money to do exactly that. But the support of Justin and my other team members convinced me that it was worth carrying on. And eventually the agency gained a reputation for being slightly different and customers found their way to us in growing numbers.

However, the doors of Oakhill weren't just open to estate-agency clients.

A couple of times a week I'd get a visitor who needed something other than my estate-agency services. People who had known me as a tearaway kid now saw me as a businessman making a success of himself. I was a walking example of the possibility of change.

'Go and see Michael,' they advised other young people who were struggling with drink and drugs, or just with the unfairness that comes hand in hand with being born poor. I helped whenever I could, regularly taking men with alcohol issues along to a local men's meeting. It didn't work for all of them, but those who got it grabbed the chance to do things differently.

I took the twelfth step – that I should spend the rest of my life helping others – very seriously. Along with sticking by my ethos of honesty – which won Oakhill the best estate-agent award in Isleworth for five years running – I made sure that Oakhill was a proper part of the local community, supporting local fundraising initiatives, giving back whenever possible. It was just part of the way I had to live. And the truth was, it made me feel good.

33

Getting sober was great for my professional life but it was hard on my personal life. Without Hayley, I missed having someone special to share the good times with. I occasionally went to mixed meetings but I knew that the last thing I needed was a relationship with someone else in recovery – that is, any relationship deeper than a friendship. Too many complications. I still went clubbing with my friends, drinking soft drinks while they drank enough alcohol to make them brave enough to dance or talk to strangers.

I did meet women on those nights out that I ended up in bed with, but I found it difficult to make the transition from sex to anything more serious. I was still learning how to be open and honest in all my interactions. It was all too easy to accidentally mislead the women I met and leave them disappointed.

Shortly before I set up my own business, I went on a night out with some colleagues. Kelly came up to me at the bar. My being sober intrigued her and soon we were chatting. I offered to walk her home. She was good fun and beautiful. I enjoyed her company and asked her on a proper date. At the end of a great evening I stayed the night.

Kelly and I had a good time together but it was clear to me pretty quickly that we weren't going to be together for the long run. The quiet way I wanted to live my life wouldn't suit her. Like Hayley, Kelly lived to party. She liked to go out. She had lots of friends. I suspected that she went on a lot of dates. We parted amiably and said we would see each other around, though I secretly thought that was the last we would see of each other.

A couple of months later, I was persuaded to go out again. I wasn't expecting much of the evening but fate had other plans.

I was standing by the bar with a group of friends when I saw a woman who made my heart leap out of my chest. She must have felt me looking at her. She turned to catch my eye and her eyes began to crinkle in amusement when she caught me staring at her so openly. When she smiled, it lit up her whole face. I knew I had to talk to her.

Her name was Sacha, she said. That evening, she was out with some girlfriends from work. She worked for Virgin Atlantic. Long-haul cabin crew. First class. Her career had taken her all over the world. The previous week she'd been in Los Angeles. Next she would be off to Johannesburg. Her travels gave her a sophistication that made me nervous. I wasn't a shy man by any means but Sacha was a goddess. And she had a boyfriend.

'We've been together for a while,' she said.

I hated him immediately. Who was he? How did he get so lucky? What did he have that I didn't?

'But maybe we could meet for lunch?' Sacha suggested. 'As friends.'

I jumped at the chance. As friends? I knew what that really meant. She was interested.

So I got her number and found out when she would next be in the UK. We made a plan. A fortnight later, we met for lunch and she opened up to me about the boyfriend she'd been with for seven years.

'We were kids when we met. I think we're growing apart,' she said. But she was still clear that she didn't want to get involved in anything else until she'd sorted that situation out. I appreciated and admired her honesty, though I wished more than anything that she'd sort the situation out sooner rather than later.

After that first lunch, Sacha contacted me via Facebook. I was delighted to see her name among the messages. It was still complicated, however. She was travelling with work. She had the situation with her boyfriend to sort out. In the meantime, I was facing a new and unexpected 'situation' of my own.

'I'm pregnant.'

Kelly came straight out with it. She cradled her tiny bump protectively as she waited for me to respond. But I was lost for words. 'It's yours,' she prompted.

'How do you know?' I said, hating myself for the bluntness of my response.

Her face dropped.

'I'm not asking you to marry me, Michael,' she said. 'I just want you to be there for the baby.'

'If it is my baby,' I blundered on. 'Look, if it is mine, of course I'll be there for it but—'

'It's yours.' Kelly turned her face away from me. I felt my heart sink to my boots. All my life I had fantasized about what it would be like to have a father who was there for me, and here I was already turning away from my own child before it was even born.

I tried to justify my feelings. I hadn't seen Kelly in months. When I met her, I thought she was seeing other men as well as me. Now she was back with a baby bump, and just as I'd met the woman I thought might be the love of my life.

And it looked as though Sacha felt the same way about me. In her last message she'd hinted that she was planning to break up with her boyfriend next time she was back in the UK.

But now this.

Kelly sat down heavily. She sighed. I could tell that this baby had been as much of a surprise to her as it was to me. She hadn't planned to trap me into anything by getting pregnant. She hadn't even told me as soon as she knew but waited until she worked out how she felt.

I reached out and took her hand.

'I'll be there for you both,' I said.

The news that Kelly was pregnant changed everything. I decided I couldn't keep flirting with Sacha until Kelly and I had worked out what we were going to do. She was going to keep the baby. There was no doubt about that. And if the child was mine, I would do everything I could to help raise him or her. I was firm that once the baby was born, there would have to be a DNA test. For us to jam together a family unit based on a lie would not work for any of us. Not Kelly, not me and not the baby.

Sacha must have guessed that something was going on from

my short, distracted answers. She stopped messaging me as frequently as she had been. I missed getting her messages, which had never failed to put a smile on my face. Though she was no longer writing to me, I kept checking her profile, seeing where she was flying. Jealously clicking through the photos she posted of nights out in exotic places. Trying to work out if the blokes in the pictures she posted were just friends or potential lovers. It was driving me nuts.

Meanwhile, I did my best to be supportive to Kelly. I read up on caring for newborns. I tried to get her everything she needed. I wished every day that I could be in love with Kelly and not Sacha. I wished that everything would work out for the best.

After what felt like forever, my daughter Connie finally arrived in the summer of 2011. I knew the moment I saw her that we weren't going to need a DNA test. This was my little girl. She blinked at me with familiar eyes. I held her, so tiny in my hands, and my heart swelled with love for her right away. It was a feeling stronger than anything I had expected. I kissed her little forehead and thanked the universe for this perfect twist of fate.

When I got back home from the hospital that night, I logged on to Facebook. The message icon was lit up. I opened it to find a message from Sacha. I hadn't heard from her in months. Her timing was incredible. I read her message, which was full of news about her adventures all over the world. She'd be back in the UK that weekend. She was wondering if I was interested in having lunch again, now that her boyfriend was old news. Assuming I hadn't got myself a new woman in the meantime!

There was a new woman in my life but not in the way Sacha

might have expected. I knew that I had to write to her and tell her what was really going on. So I went for it.

'This morning,' I wrote, 'I held my baby girl for the first time.'

It wasn't the best way to start a relationship. I didn't think Sacha would be interested once she heard I was a new father, even if I wasn't in a relationship with Kelly anymore. Who needs that level of complication? But to my amazement, Sacha wrote back to me. She said she was glad to find out what was really going on with me, having spent the past few months assuming that I wasn't interested in her, despite the fact that it was obvious on the couple of times we'd met that we had some serious chemistry going on – physical and emotional. She'd sent that message as a last-ditch attempt, and she couldn't let that sort of connection go. But how were we going to move forward now?

It's no understatement to say I had a lot going on. I did my best to help Kelly with Connie. I would be there as often as I could.

I had been concerned that fatherhood wouldn't come naturally and I still worried now. Was I getting it right? Was I holding Connie properly? Was I talking to her in the best way? Should I be singing to her more? I had no idea. After all, what examples did I have to refer to? My two paternal role models had been absent (Dad) or distant and disciplinarian (Pete). I wanted to be a different kind of father. One who could be relied upon no matter what. One who would never frighten the baby I held in my arms or leave her alone to face a difficult world.

Meanwhile, Sacha and I began dating quietly. She seemed

to understand that I needed to take things slowly. We went to dinner as a couple for the first time. To Nando's. It wasn't exactly the kind of fancy place Sacha deserved but it's an evening that sticks in my memory because it felt so right. I'd been honest with Sacha from the start and she still wanted to be with me. That was a revelation.

As Connie grew, so did my love for her. Every time I saw her my heart swelled a little more. I didn't know I could love someone so much. I was utterly besotted by this little bundle. I never thought I would feel that way.

It made me wonder how Dad had felt about me. Had he ever held me and looked down into my sleeping face and made the sort of promises I made to Connie every day? How did he feel when he broke those promises? Had there ever been a moment when he might have done things differently? When he might have made the decision to try to overcome his addiction for me?

I tried to imagine what Dad would be like as a grandfather. He hadn't met Connie. I wondered if he ever would. I didn't even know where he was.

34

Dad was still an addict. In fact, he was almost an ex-addict, though not by design. I was at work one day when Mum rang to say she'd had a call from my Auntie Kathy, Dad's sister, to say that Dad was in hospital in intensive care. The person who spoke to Mum suggested that this was likely to be the end of the road. If Mum, Maria or I wanted to see Dad again, we had best come now.

I left work at once and went to the hospital with Mum and Maria, dreading what we would see there. Dad was unconscious, hooked up to a huge array of machines that were doing the breathing for him. Mum clutched my hand as we waited to see him.

When we were allowed into the room, Maria and I sat on chairs while Mum stood next to the bed. She lifted one of Dad's hands, the one that didn't have tubes coming out of the back of it, and held it tenderly. She stroked the hair back from his face and even kissed his forehead. It was the first time I'd seen her be properly affectionate to him. While the machines beeped in the background, I struggled to hold in my own tears. My sister sat on the other side of Dad's bed and we both watched our parents share this strange, tender moment. It was probably the closest we would ever get to a happy family reunion.

I had known that hospital visit was going to be hard for us all but I had no idea how hard until we came out of ICU and into the waiting room again.

There were two women, both of them about Maria's age, sitting on the plastic chairs, waiting to be allowed in to visit. Allowed in to visit *their* dad.

My dad was their dad.

It wasn't just me, Mum and Maria who were clueless. The two women who turned out to be my half-sisters hadn't met each other before that moment either. They had different mums. They'd grown up in different parts of the city. They hadn't any idea about each other's existence. Or about mine or Maria's. Or that their beloved dad was still married to Theresa Maughan at the time he romanced both their mothers. Auntie Kathy had tracked them down via social media.

If Maria and I were shocked to meet our new siblings, Mum was devastated. Those two women had been conceived at the same time as Maria, when Mum recklessly let Dad – her husband – back into her heart after months spent on the run from him.

As a result of Dad ending up in ICU that day, we found out that he had thirteen children in all, including Maria and me. His sister Kathy had worked it all out and Dad would confirm it when he finally came round.

The stories my newly found half-sisters told me fitted with my and Maria's experience. It wasn't that Dad had abandoned me and Maria for a new family. He had shirked his responsibility for all thirteen of us. We later discovered that not one of us had received so much as a birthday card. None of us really knew him at all.

Yet, hearing that he was ill had brought four of us running to be with him. The power of our longing for a connection was far stronger than Dad deserved. Blood really was thicker than water in the case of Kevin Wright and his kids.

Despite the hospital's dire predictions, Dad recovered. He was discharged from hospital to a hostel and carried on just as before, leaving us siblings struggling to piece together what it all meant.

It was a difficult time. If I'd felt sad about my lack of a relationship with Dad before, knowing that he'd had the same lack of relationship with twelve other people didn't help. Until then, I'd been confident that I could be a different kind of dad, but hearing about my other siblings shook me. A couple of them were addicts, just as Dad was. Just as I had been and still was at heart. Did we really stand a chance of escaping the same fate? Would I wake up one morning and decide I could no longer be bothered to live the life I'd worked so hard to create? Would my genetic inheritance overcome everything I'd learned?

At the meetings, people tried to tell me otherwise. All I had to do was take things day by day, they reminded me. Keep working the steps. Keep knowing that the sanity I had achieved was a far better feeling than the fleeting high offered by cocaine, heroin, alcohol or meaningless sex.

I remembered what Matt said when my attempt to make

amends with the dealer I'd turned over didn't go as planned and I feared he would come after me.

'God didn't save you from drowning so you could be kicked to death on the beach.'

I'd had some dark times. Moments when I thought I couldn't carry on. But at each of those moments someone had appeared to hold my hand and lead me forwards through the fog. I'd survived a suicide attempt and beatings. I'd never overdosed, though I'd often come close. Someone somewhere had my back.

And now I had a more compelling reason than ever to stay sober and clean.

Connie.

She needed me just as I had needed my dad. It wasn't inevitable that I would let her down. I could be there for her. I could be the one to break the pattern of neglect and abuse that ran through my family like the genes for brown hair and blue eyes. I could do things differently.

I made arrangements with Kelly that I would take Connie every other weekend. When she wasn't with me, she would always be able to find me. I would always be available to talk whenever she wanted to. I was determined that she would never have to wonder if I really loved her. She would always know she was right there, in the middle of my heart.

By now Sacha and I were living together. While I did my best to be a good father, Sacha threw herself into the role of stepmother. She took to Connie immediately. It made me teary to see how close they were. Sacha showed that it was possible to be a good step-parent, investing as much love in Connie as she would in a child of her own.

When Sacha told me that she was pregnant, my reaction was entirely different to the first time I'd heard those words. I didn't panic this time. I was nervous but I was also excited. Connie was going to have a little sister.

35

Once upon a time, I was the kid the police officers in Richmond and Isleworth most wanted to see banged up for good. More than a decade later, some of those same officers still patrolled the streets around my estate agency. Some of them were almost friends now. They stopped to talk. They asked about how business was going and about my little girl. I think they were amused to see how much a part of the local establishment I'd become. It was all very friendly, but there was still a part of me that was always waiting for the atmosphere to change.

That year, 2014, was to be a year full of changes for me. In January, Sacha gave birth to our baby, Sienna, a sister for Connie. Holding Sienna in my hands for the first time, all the feelings I'd had when I first held Connie came rushing back. I could hardly believe that this tiny baby was my little girl. I promised to look after her for the rest of my days. Connie peered into her sister's cot and I knew they would be the best of friends.

Around the time Sienna was born, there was an article in the local newspaper asking Isleworth residents if they knew of a local resident who'd gone above and beyond for the community. I read the piece one lunchtime and didn't think any more of it. I'd forgotten all about it when I received a letter from

Hounslow Council, inviting me to an award ceremony at the Civic Centre. Someone had seen that article in the paper and nominated me!

At first I told myself it was some kind of wind-up. I asked my brother what he thought. When he saw the letter, he said he thought it looked legit to him. Why would someone go to the bother of faking a letter from the council for a laugh? He thought I should go.

I still wasn't sure. The awards were for 'Community Heroes' and I couldn't see how I fitted that category. Surely all the trouble and anguish I'd caused all over the community as a teenager still outweighed the effort I was making now?

'Just go,' my brother said.

The ceremony was scheduled for a weekday evening. I didn't bother to ask anyone to go with me. I was pretty certain that at best I would be one of dozens of nominees that day. It wasn't worth asking anyone to take the time to come along. Sacha had her hands full with the new baby and with Connie, who was staying with us for a couple of days.

On the day of the ceremony I had a ton of work to get through. As the time I would need to leave drew closer, I still had letters to write and calls to make. I could have used another couple of hours at my desk. I almost didn't go to the ceremony at all.

'Michael Maisey.'

When my name was called, my mouth dropped open in surprise. I stood up and looked around the room. It was packed with so many people who seemed like they deserved the award more. Even as I walked up to the stage, I was expecting the compère to lean into the microphone and say, 'Only joking, Michael. You can sit back down.'

But that didn't happen. I made it to the stage, applauded all the way by this room full of people who didn't seem to think it was a joke.

I tried hard not to show how nervous I was feeling as I was given my award by the chief superintendent of the Metropolitan Police. The last time such a high-ranking police officer had spoken to me was almost twenty years earlier, when I was pulled in for the corner-shop robbery gone wrong. The words of that earlier lecture from the chief superintendent came back to me as I stepped up to shake the chief super's hand, man to man.

You're in danger of wasting your life, Maisey. You're in danger of spending years bouncing in and out of prison. You'll end up with nothing. No job, no family, no self-respect. No life.

'Congratulations, Michael,' said the chief super now. 'Well deserved.'

He kept his hand on my shoulder as we posed for the photographers. When the flashing lights didn't wake me up, I finally began to trust that this wasn't a dream after all.

I was sad then that I hadn't invited anyone along to support me. It was the first time in my life that I'd won an award and no one I loved was there to see it happen. Everyone else had brought along their families and friends. They were with them all the way, cheering and applauding as they went up on stage. I was on my own.

Perhaps it wasn't just because I'd thought the awards ceremony would be a waste of time. Perhaps it was because, though I had worked hard to be a different person, the truth was I still couldn't quite believe I deserved my second chance.

Sitting back down, I held my certificate in my hand and looked at it as though I was expecting to see someone else's name written on it, as though I thought that at any minute, someone would take it from me and say, 'Sorry, Michael. We made a mistake. This isn't meant for you.'

I felt very alone in that crowded room. I watched the eight other nominees take to the stage and smile with the pride they deserved to have in their achievements. I just wanted the ceremony to end so that I could slip out through the back door and go home.

However, when it finished, I found I couldn't get away as easily as I hoped. All the nominees were invited to a little reception afterwards. I wasn't getting out of it. One of the ceremony's organizers took me by the arm and told me that there were people who wanted to meet me. The chief superintendent wanted the chance to get to know me better.

Feeling strangely nervous again, I followed the organizer to a corner of the room where a group of dignitaries were deep in conversation. I was astonished when the little circle parted to allow me inside. The chief super asked me to tell my story. As I told these strangers how my childhood had been and where my teenage years had taken me, I felt the energy change from shock, to empathy, to pride.

'Michael is exactly the kind of role model kids round here need,' the super told them.

After I shared this story I thanked them for my award and told them I had to go due to me having a newborn at home. As I walked away I couldn't help feel a little sad. Everyone was celebrating and drinking champagne with family and friends and here I was on a cold winter's evening leaving on my own. But I knew my worth as a man in this world didn't count on this award, or on celebrating it; it counted on me being better than the men that went before me in my family history. That night it was as simple as going home and being supportive to my partner and children.

Sacha was in the living room giving Sienna a feed.

'How was it?' she asked.

'Good,' I said. 'Good.'

Connie was already in bed. I quietly stepped into her bedroom and snuck a look at her sleeping. I kissed my fingertips and pressed the kiss to Connie's forehead, careful not to wake her.

'I love you, little one,' I whispered.

Then I went back to Sacha and took over Sienna's feed. As she settled into my arms, Sienna looked at me with her big, innocent eyes and I felt my heart melt a little more.

It was one of the best nights of my life. All the more so because this was a moment I had never expected to have. All those nights in Feltham, struggling, fantasizing about a better life, all of the pain I went through, I couldn't even have conceived of a life that felt this good. I had never felt so content, so happy and so loved. I had Sacha, I had my daughters, I had a home, a career, great friends. I even had the respect of the chief superintendent of the Metropolitan Police, something I never thought would be of any interest to me at all, but as I have grown and changed it feels nice to be accepted and appreciated for the work I have done to both help others and better myself.

I kissed Sienna's forehead and told her I loved her, just like I loved her big sister. She finished feeding and I rocked her to sleep. Once again, I promised her and Connie that I would always be there for them. I would be the dad I wished I'd had. Things could be different. They already were.

Epilogue

I am the man I am today because of the people I met along the way. For better or worse, they helped to shape me and I am grateful to every one of them for the lessons they helped me to learn. A watershed moment for me was when I started to understand that I wasn't born bad. Life chipped away at me and moulded me into an angry, scared young man. I applied this same understanding to all the people in my life, even the people who hurt me. Inevitably they too had been hurt in their turn. We were all children once, relying on the adults who were supposed to love and care for us. Considering this helped me to find peace and forgiveness.

So what happened to the people you've met in these pages?

Mum is still living in Isleworth. She's been sober for over eighteen years and is still going to meetings. We have a good relationship now and she regularly visits me, Sacha and her granddaughters. We've talked a lot about what was going to be in this book and it's helped us come to a greater under-standing of what happened when Maria and I were small. I understand now that Mum's own childhood left her ill-prepared for being a mother. She had so much pain of her own to deal with after the abuse she suffered in her family, in the children's home and in her relationship with my dad. At the same time she had none of the professional support that might have helped her see that drinking was not the way to keep that pain away.

Mum's recently been told that she will receive compensation for the abuse she and her siblings suffered in the Nazareth home back in Ireland. It's too late for Uncle Tommy, of course, but hopefully for the rest of the Maughan children this recognition of their suffering will make a difference.

In the past few years, Mum has blossomed. I am so proud of the woman she has become. I love her so much. She has truly turned her life around.

Dad's still around. He's still an addict. We see each other from time to time and, while I know he's pleased with the way I'm navigating my recovery, I don't think there's much hope that seeing me clean and sober will encourage him to get clean himself. After that time he ended up in ICU after the overdose, I did actually persuade him to come with me to one twelve-step meeting. He said it wasn't for him. As far as I know, he's never been to another.

Dad lives in a single room in a large house with other addicts. He keeps the curtains closed all day while he watches TV, existing on a diet of cereal, Nutella and bread. He is still estranged from most of his family. Of his thirteen children, I am the only one who really keeps in touch with him now.

It's sad and painful watching my father slowly decay due to his addictions. We have spoken about funeral arrangements and every time I see him it feels like it might be a last goodbye, but I tell him I love him regularly and he tells me how proud he is of me. Just to hear him say that means more to me than he can ever know.

Unfortunately, Mum and my stepdad Pete are getting

divorced. I'm still in contact with Pete. He lives in Hampton now. When I talked to him about my childhood and the relationship he and I had back then, he told me that his main recollection was that he was overwhelmed. He had no experience of parenting when he inherited Maria and me. He loved Mum but her drinking and its impact on her health were a huge worry. There were times when Pete was basically on his own with four kids. Like Mum, Pete did his best. He's a great man and I'm grateful for all that he did for us.

I still hear from Mary from time to time. I keep the prayer cards she used to send me while I was in prison. Mary moved away from Isleworth after her son, who had joined a gang, was stabbed and nearly killed. Gang violence is an increasing problem in south-west London.

The one thing Mary taught me was that faith is important. She had faith in me and it feels like her prayers have worked at last. I will always be grateful for her love and support.

Ivan, my old partner in crime, did four years in prison on the attempted murder charge that landed us both in Feltham when we were teens. Since then, he's been in and out of prison multiple times, spending the best part of fourteen years behind bars. However, when we caught up right after his last release, he seemed different. When I asked him what had changed, he told me that while serving his last sentence he took part in the RAPt programme and started to get into twelve-step recovery. Though he hasn't stayed entirely sober, looking at his life through the twelve-step lens has had a long-lasting effect. It's two years since he was last inside. That's the longest time he has spent out of prison since we were teens. The last time we saw each other he told me he was determined never to go back inside again. He has a baby on the way with his old childhood sweetheart Kelly.

He also told me that he'd seen Samuel Larye, the solicitor who worked so hard to get me and Ivan off. He's retired now. He deserves a very happy old age!

I don't know what happened to Dredd. I never him saw him again after I got out of Feltham the first time. I hope he's doing well. I don't know how I would have got through my first stay in prison without him. I might not even be alive if he hadn't alerted the guards to the fact I was being attacked by Pepsi and his mates.

I haven't seen Pepsi since then either. I don't bear him a grudge. I don't know what his family background was, but I don't suppose his life outside Feltham was a bed of roses. I wish him only happiness.

I saw Mason, who pretended to be my cousin so we could share a cell, a couple of years ago on the street in Isleworth. I hadn't seen him since I got out of Feltham at the end of that stretch. He was in a bad way. Still addicted to heroin. It broke my heart to see my old mate looking so ill.

I took him to a cafe and bought him something to eat. He said he was pleased to hear how well I was doing. He didn't seem interested in his own recovery. I can only hope some day he finds a way through.

Sean, who reached out to me in that Belfast meeting and set me on the road to sanity, is still sober. It's been almost forty years for him now. He's helped hundreds, if not thousands of men to turn their lives around.

I'm grateful to Sean for guiding me through the early stages of the twelve-step programme. I'm grateful too to the programme itself for providing a framework for the changes I needed to make and for nudging me towards a better relationship with my higher power – God, as I choose to call it.

Hayley, my first love, the woman who got me through some of the toughest years of my life, didn't want to stay in touch after we broke up. That's understandable, although it's sometimes difficult to accept. I would have loved to remain friends but it was hard for both of us back when we split. We didn't have the emotional tools to salvage a friendship from what we had.

Maybe one day Hayley and I will sit down and laugh about all the mad things we did growing up. She'll always have a place in my heart. In the meantime, I wish her only the best. She deserves it.

Hayley's parents, Steve and Caroline, were also right there for me when I began to make the changes that have brought me to where I am today. They encouraged me in so many ways with their humbling persistence and patience. I will always be grateful for the way they took me into their family and did their best to help.

As for me? Well, I'm still sober. On 15 December 2017, I celebrated a whole decade without a drink or drugs. That Christmas party in Belfast where I got so drunk I attacked my boss and broke into Hayley's boss's house turned out to be the last time I would ever touch alcohol.

My estate agency is still flourishing. Despite my being told that running an estate agency in an honest way wouldn't work, Oakhill has gone on to win best estate agent in Isleworth for five years running now, based on our happy customer reviews. We're not the biggest estate agent's and I'll probably never be a millionaire, but that's not what motivates me. What motivates me is having proper values and treating people fairly, with honesty.

Perhaps my dream of changing the world's view of estate agents was a little ambitious but I would like to think I've made a difference in the Isleworth area at least.

And now I'm working on fulfilling another old ambition. My dream of becoming an actor, which was cut short when I was eleven, has started to come true again. I have recently starred in four short films. I even played Jack the Ripper in a television documentary about his life. Other projects are in the pipeline. But acting isn't a means of running away from myself anymore. I'm finally comfortable with who I am, and when I take off the costume and make-up I wear for any role, I'm happy to be myself again.

I'm proud to say that neither of my daughters has ever seen me touch alcohol or drugs. I'll toast their eighteenth birthdays with elderflower cordial! But I know that being a good father goes beyond not drinking or using; I am there for my daughters not just physically but emotionally. I do my best to hear them, to support them and nurture them. Learning to parent properly has been an area of massive growth in my life. Of course, it helps that I have a wonderful partner and co-parent in Sacha.

A couple of years ago, Sacha and I decided it was time to leave London; we wanted a better way of life for Sienna and Connie, and my old dream of owning a house in the country with lots of land was calling. We moved to a house in the Blackdown Hills, on the edge of Devon, with ten acres. I wanted somewhere I could host men's retreats, based around the kind of healing I needed myself. I invited twenty men to attend the inaugural retreat in September 2018. We challenged ourselves both physically and emotionally, with time in a Native American-style sweat lodge and Wim Hof breathing exercises.

On the evening that I celebrated a decade of sobriety, I asked Sacha to marry me. She's supported me and stood by me through my journey in recovery. She's a great mum to Sienna and a wonderful stepmum to Connie. I am blessed to have some truly wonderful women in my life. Angels. Sacha has been nothing less than an angel to me. We got married in the autumn of 2018, with Connie and Sienna as bridesmaids. I can't wait to spend the rest of my life with her.

I still go to schools and prisons to talk about my recovery through twelve-step fellowships and The Forward Trust, formerly known as RAPt.

The Forward Trust boasts some impressive results. Compared to prisoners who don't have access to The Forward Trust's support, those who take part are 65 per cent less likely to reoffend.

There are hundreds of people in recovery who would be happy to volunteer to share their experiences through The Forward Trust. Unfortunately, as I discovered myself, the prison service does not have the resources to take advantage of these people and their dedication. It's not easy to find people with the flexibility to chair a meeting in a prison during the working week, so it's especially frustrating to get those people together only to find that, upon turning up, the prison doesn't have enough guards to enable the meeting to be run. It happened to me on two occasions when I was supposed to be chairing a meeting at High Down.

We need to look at the way we're sentencing young kids. Is prison really the right answer? And if prison is the right answer, then how can we make sure that the time young offenders spend inside is used to help them lead better lives on the outside. They're literally a captive audience. Instead of keeping them in a cell for twenty-three hours a day, why aren't we diverting resources into their education and proper psychological support? Why aren't we educating them about the things that really matter? Relationships? Communication? How to be a good partner or a good dad? We need to give them the tools to be self-sufficient on the outside, to enable them to look at the gang lifestyle and say it's not for them. We need to educate our young men that health and happiness are much more important than wealth.

When I chaired my first meeting in Feltham, Elijah, the lad who came up to me afterwards, told me he related to everything I'd said. He expressed how much he wanted to change, but he had so little hope for himself he couldn't imagine taking the steps I had to make things different.

That day, I told him where I went to meetings, which wasn't far from where he lived. A couple of years later, I saw him on the outside as I was on my way to the meeting I'd told him about. I pulled over and, despite him being surrounded by a large group of friends all doing their best to look hard, he recognized me immediately and greeted me with a hug. We spoke for a few minutes and he introduced me to his mates. I asked him what he was doing. He said he was back to his old ways. He'd been released back to a community where nobody has much, to parents who didn't really care and friends who all lived the same way of life: existing on the edges of society, numbing their worries with substance abuse.

I encouraged Elijah to come with me to the meeting but he had already had a few drinks and declined. I gave him my number but never heard from him again.

I feel really sad about this. I look at our prison service and the prison population constantly on the rise and the most obvious cause seems to be the lack of role models for our young men.

Elijah, if you're reading this book, I'm still here for you. I'm here for all of you, young men and old, locked up and struggling with addiction.

You are the reason I wrote this book. I could have ridden off into the sunset with my partner and kids. I could have said I don't want the world knowing my story and judging me for my past. What will my children think? Maybe they will get teased in school about what is written within these pages? Maybe my business reputation will be tarnished?

But what's more important here? Me or the thousands upon thousands of men looking for a role model, and their families, and the families affected by the crimes they commit? They need to hear from someone who has been where they have been and has turned it around.

That's what's more important, and if my children get teased at school, I will be there to support them. And if I get judged, then I get judged. It's OK. I can't please everyone.

It wasn't easy writing this book, but I did it for you, for all those suffering.

I have a dream that one day, if people have to go to prison once, we will do such a good job of rehabilitating them and supporting them through their sentence that once released they will never go back again. Their lives will be improved, not ruined. I have a dream that the tools I have used to combat my own mental demons can be passed on to anyone else battling mental health, and that suicide will become a thing of the past. I have a dream that we will overcome bullying in schools all over the world by having open and honest conversations about the long-term effects it has on the victims and the perpetrators.

This book is the first step towards achieving that goal for me, and I will continue to do all I can to help men and women who need help.

My message in its essence is essentially this:

It's possible.

It is possible to go through more shit and pain than you think anyone could ever take and still turn it all around and be a success. In business. In relationships with your partner and your children. In life.

To all my brothers and sisters who haven't made it yet, I wait for you here. Find me on social media or at one of my men's retreats and I will help you on your way.

With love and gratitude,

Michael Maisey

Acknowledgements

I would first like to thank my wife Sacha for standing by me through some of the most demanding and testing times of my life. Since we met when I was four years sober, you've been my rock, through the arrival of two children, setting up a business, moving house three times and the start of my acting career. All the while, you've helped me maintain my sobriety. It hasn't been an easy ride, but I am grateful that we have shared this journey together, through all the ups and downs.

I would like to thank my two beautiful children, Connie and Sienna. You continue to be my greatest teachers, showing me how to live with an open heart and how to be a GENTLE man. You both inspire me to be better every day.

A massive thank you to Chrissie Manby for helping me put this book together. Without you this wouldn't have happened. From our chance meeting in a restaurant in Bergen, Norway, to the hours spent in your house in London, to the days spent in my house in Devon going over my whole life in detail – you believed in me, and you believed in this story. I am so grateful to have met you, and for all your help. You helped breathe life into it and pieced it all together. It's been a privilege working with you.

To my agent Humfrey Hunter for believing in me, for

supporting me, for being on the end of the phone many times when I needed someone to talk to, for finding the right book deal for us, for your wisdom and for your guidance. Thank you.

Thanks to Pan Macmillan and all the team there. You're great, all of you. Especially Ingrid Connell. Thank you, Ingrid, for believing in me, for seeing something in me that maybe I didn't fully see myself. I knew from our first meeting in your offices in London, when I was feeling way out of my depth, that the publisher I wanted to sign with was yours. I told Humfrey right after our meeting. Thank you for your insight, your knowledge and your guidance that has gone way beyond the book.

To Tom Hardy. When we first met in Richmond in 2009 I was around eighteen months sober. I was still a bit lost, not knowing if I could ever really turn my life around. We spoke for a while that day and you inspired me to keep going. You helped me believe change was possible. Not only that, you inspired me to strive for more. Over the past ten years of friendship you have continually encouraged me to keep growing as a person and to keep following my dreams. I will never forget how, on that cold afternoon in March 2017, while we were kayaking on the River Thames, you urged me to believe in myself and write my story, setting off the chain of events that led to this book. I'm grateful for that, Tommy. You're a great man. Beyond the celebrity and the glitz and glamour, you're a down-to-earth, humble family man, who supports others and inspires many. I'm not sure the world always sees that side of you, so I'm honouring you for it here.

Finally, thanks to all the people from recovery meetings all over the world. From the newcomers to the old timers with years of wisdom. Thank you for the countless hours we have shared in listening, learning and growing together. I am grateful to you all.